Photoshop® Studio

with Bert Monroy

New Riders

201 West 103rd Street, Indianapolis, Indiana 46290

Photoshop Studio with Bert Monroy

International Standard Book Number: 0-7357-1246-8

Library of Congress Catalog Card Number: 2001097566

Printed in the United States of America

First Printing: July 2002

06   05   04   03   02   7   6   5   4   3   2   1

Interpretation of the printing code: The rightmost double-digit number is the year of the book's printing; the rightmost single-digit number is the number of the book's printing. For example, the printing code 02-1 shows that the first printing of the book occurred in 2002.

Trademarks

Warning and Disclaimer

Publisher
David Dwyer

Associate Publisher
Stephanie Wall

Production Manager
Gina Kanouse

Managing Editor
Sarah Kearns

Acquisitions Editor
Jody Kennen

Project Editor
Michael Thurston

Technical Editor
Dan Margulis

Copy Editor
Ginny Bess

Product Marketing Manager
Kathy Malmloff

Publicity Manager
Susan Nixon

Manufacturing Coordinator
Jim Conway

Cover Designer
Aren Howell

Interior Designer
Kim Scott, www.bumpy.com

Compositor
Kim Scott

Proofreader
Teresa Hendey

Indexer
Lisa Stumpf

Contents at a Glance

Table of Contents

About the Author

Bert Monroy was born and raised in New York City, where he spent 20 years in the advertising industry as an art director and creative director for various agencies as well as his own. Upon discovering computers with the introduction of the Macintosh 128 in 1984, he embarked on a new digital career. He embraced the computer as an artistic medium and is considered one of the pioneers of digital art. Bert's work has been seen in *MacWorld, MacUser, Byte, Verbum, Computer Artist, MacWeek*, and the comic book *Shatter*, to mention a few. His work has also been featured in scores of books including *Making Art on a Macintosh, The Photoshop WOW Book, The Illustrator WOW Book, The Art of Digital Painting, The Grey Book*, and *Photoshop A to Z* in Japan. His work has also been used to introduce many software products, such as VideoWorks (predecessor to Director), PixelPaint, SoundCap, and ImageStudio.

Bert was a founding partner in the New York firm Incredible Interactivity, which was responsible for interactive multimedia presentations as early as 1986–before the terms had been coined. Presentations were created for such clients as General Motors, American Express, and Knoll International. Bert co-authored *The Official Adobe Photoshop Handbook*, which was the first book on Photoshop and the only one for almost two years. It won various awards. He also co-authored *Adobe Photoshop: A Visual Guide to the Mac*, which was published in 14 languages, and *Photoshop 4*, published in Japan by Agosto and BNN. A current book, *Photoshop Channel CHOPS*, co-authored with David Biedny and Nathan Moody, concentrates on the most advanced features of the program that are not covered anywhere else. His most recent book, released in 2000 by New Riders, is called *Bert Monroy: Photorealistic Techniques with Photoshop and Illustrator*. It concentrates on the techniques he has established over the years in the creation of his fine art works. It is available at Amazon.com. Bert is an accomplished teacher and lecturer who has served on the faculty of The School of Visual Arts (NYC), Center for Creative Imaging (ME), Dynamic Graphics Educational Foundation (IL), and California College of Arts & Crafts (CA), and lectures at many other institutions and conferences around the world. He currently teaches at San Francisco State University. Bert now lives in Berkeley, California. He continues to serve his installed base of clients, which include Apple Computer, Adobe Systems, Pioneer Electronics, Fujitsu, SONY, AT&T, Chevron, and American Express. Bert has also done a considerable amount of film work for Industrial Light & Magic, Pacific Data Images, and R/Greenberg Association.

Acknowledgments

There are many people I wish to thank who were instrumental in my efforts to publish this book. There are many who must be mentioned by virtue of the fact that because of them I got to write any book.

There's a great bunch of folks at New Riders that deserve tremendous appreciation for an outstanding job. Thanks go to Chris Nelson, David Dwyer, and Steve Weiss. Their continued support and friendship keeps me writing for New Riders. Special thanks to Jody Kennen, who tried to keep me on schedule and was so forgiving when I wasn't. To the design team and all the rest of the NRP folks, my heartfelt thanks.

My wife Zosia deserves a big hand for putting up with my long hours. She also met the deadlines I imposed on her as my first line of defense proofreader. She got the first draft that came right from my head and fingers and somehow made it sound like English.

Big thanks to Dan Margulis; his expertise and editing were crucial in producing a book I could be proud of. His frankness is and always will be appreciated. His friendship is relished.

Jeff Schewe for making me look good in my portrait.

My friend John C. Dvorak for his kind words.

Now come the personal thank yous.

My high school buddy, John Melo—if it wasn't for him, I never would have pursued a career in art.

John and Tom Knoll for dreaming up Photoshop and making it happen.

Thanks to the folks at Adobe for picking up where John and Tom left off. I also want to thank them for putting out so many other great software packages. In this group, special thanks go to Mark Hamburg, Marc Pawliger, Chris Cox, and Sandra Alves. I can't forget Karen Gauthier and Julieanne Kost because they add so much fun to working with Adobe. Also part of this group but with added features, Russell Brown and his wife Jan.

The folks at Apple for putting out a machine that got me hooked into computers in the first place. There are a few folks that deserve special thanks and they are Greg "Joz" Joswiak, David Baker, Glenn Fisher, and Phil Schiller. Glenn recently moved on to pursue new endeavors.

To Burton Holmes and the folks at WACOM for providing wonderful products that are attached to all my machines.

David Biedny, who has co-authored so many books with me.

To Leo and Pat and all the rest of the folks at TechTV for all the fun every month.

My kids, Sean and Erika, who somehow managed to turn into wonderful adults that I can consider friends.

My mother, if it wasn't for her this book would be blank.

My sisters Diana and Irene because they're cool. Their husbands Richie and Fred and all the kids for the same reason.

My good friend Bill Schoenberg, for those great hikes that gave me the badly needed break from the grind.

I definitely want to thank Mark, my nephew on my wife's side, for all the diversions. Chris, Marks' brother, because he's a good friend. My sister-in-law Iza, because she's so entertaining.

Since I entered the digital realm, I have had the immense pleasure of meeting so many wonderful people. They all need to be thanked for something or other. I can't name them all so if I missed you here, don't sweat it, you're in my heart. The Berkeley crowd, you know who you are. Cathy Abes, Bill Atkinson, Bob Bowen, Tony Bove and Cheryl Rhodes and the boys, Steve Broback, Dan Brown, Matt Brown, Casey, Luanne Cohen, Sandee Cohen, Frank Colin, Linnea Dayton, Jack Davis, John Dvorak,

Mark Drury, Katrin Eismann and John Macintosh, Diane Fenster and Miles, Bruce Fraser, Michael Gosney, Thea Grigsby and her husband Steven, Steve Guttman and Jenny and the kids, Michael Hanes, Jerry Harris and family, Tom Hedges and family, Helene, Ichiro Hirose and family, Stephan Johnson, Yoshinori Kaizu, Scott Kelby and all the folks at the NAPP, Kenn Krasner, Bob Levitus, the Linde brothers Peter and Bruce, Ray Lonsdale, Jim Ludtke, Keith McGreggor and family, Paul Mavrides, Deke McClelland, Steve Mitchell and Judy, Nathan Moody, Stanley Mouse, Walter O'Brien, Cher Pendarvis and Steve, Howard Penner, Carol Person, Ron Rick and family, Tom Rielly, Anders Ronnblom, Paul Rosenfeld, Nancy Ruenzel and all the folks at PeachPit Press, Todd Rundgren and his wife Michelle, David Schargel, Stuart Sharpe and family, Sharon Steuer and Jeff, Fran Stiles, Robin Williams and family, Colin Wood, Mark Wood and Becky and the girls, Mark Zimmer and family, all the folks at SFSU, everybody that was at CCI, and everybody at The School of Visual Arts. Love you all!

Last but certainly not the least, I want to thank all my students and the attendees of my seminars for all the ooohs and aahhhs that have always made it so much fun.

A Message from New Riders

As the reader of this book, you are our most important critic and commentator. We value your opinion and want to know what we're doing right, what we could do better, in what areas you'd like to see us publish, and any other words of wisdom you're willing to pass our way.

As Associate Publisher at New Riders, I welcome your comments. You can fax, email, or write me directly to let me know what you did or didn't like about this book—as well as what we can do to make our books better. When you write, please be sure to include this book's title, ISBN, and author, as well as your name and phone or fax number. I will carefully review your comments and share them with the authors and editors who worked on the book.

Please note that I cannot help you with technical problems related to the topic of this book, and that due to the high volume of email I receive, I might not be able to reply to every message. Thanks.

Fax   317-581-4663

Email: stephanie.wall@newriders.com

Mail: Stephanie Wall
        Associate Publisher
        New Riders Publishing
        201 West 103rd Street
        Indianapolis, IN 46290 USA

Visit Our Web Site: www.newriders.com

On our web site, you'll find information about our other books, the authors we partner with, book updates and file downloads, promotions, discussion boards for online interaction with other users and with technology experts, and a calendar of trade shows and other professional events with which we'll be involved. We hope to see you around.

Email Us from Our Web Site

Go to www.**newriders.com** and click on the Contact Us link if you...

- Have comments or questions about this book.

- Want to report errors that you have found in this book.

- Have a book proposal or are interested in writing for New Riders.

- Would like us to send you one of our author kits.

- Are an expert in a computer topic or technology and are interested in being a reviewer or technical editor.

- Want to find a distributor for our titles in your area.

- Are an educator/instructor who wants to preview New Riders books for classroom use. In the body/comments area, include your name, school, department, address, phone number, office days/hours, text currently in use, and enrollment in your department, along with your request for either desk/examination copies or additional information.

Foreword

by John C. Dvorak

The Next Great Step

Since the beginning of the desktop computing revolution in the mid 1970's, only a handful of programs have turned the small computer into a powerful productivity tool that has slowly evolved into something that the world cannot do without. Adobe Photoshop is one of those programs. Professional photographers and illustrators rely on this product to produce and modify their works in ways that were simply impossible just a few years ago. Photoshop is now a requirement in most art schools across the country. Even amateurs who are just getting into digital photography lust for their own copy of Photoshop. It is the standard editing and enhancement tool by which all others are judged. In short, it is phenomenal; it is a phenomenon.

However, unlike other applications that are sold for personal computers, this program does not stand still or rest on its laurels. Each new version of Photoshop re-invents the product, making it even more powerful and indispensable. Version 7 stays this difficult course. If the other so-called "killer applications," such as word processors, kept up with this pace of innovation, I wouldn't have to write these words, as the word processor would be doing most of the work for me. Artists were once envious of the fact that writers had these computers to themselves for a short time and could write more and better. Now it's the writers who must be envious of the artists, as the artists' toolboxes now contain Photoshop. Each iteration of Photoshop adds new features that make the artist's job easier and more efficient. Maybe I can convince Adobe to get into word processing with as much zeal.

Of course the one drawback to this fast-paced improvement is the need to learn new tricks and new ways of using an old tool. Enter Bert Monroy.

I've known Bert Monroy since the days when he created his incredible art using only a mouse and a bit-by-bit approach to his creations. Bert is one of the true pioneers in the arena of computer-aided art. He has been doing this longer than anyone I know, and his deep knowledge of Photoshop in particular is awesome. Luckily, he has the ability to explain what he knows in ways anyone can follow.

Bert's influence is such that he helps chart the course for Photoshop. Many of the new features of Photoshop are derived from his ideas, and each one is designed to make life easier for the production artist or photographer. Never forget that this is a professional tool. Just as Photoshop, the product, is the standard by which other editing products are judged, so too are Bert Monroy's books on Photoshop. No library can be complete without his books. This edition is invaluable.

Whether you're a first time Photoshop user or an old pro, you'll find this book an important addition to your library. In addition, the casual user of Photoshop can look like a pro faster than imagined by employing the carefully outlined techniques explored and explained in this book.

And know that you are part of a long history that traces back to the 1940's when early pioneers used large, old-fashioned machines to develop what was then referred to as CGI (Computer Generated Imagery). Computer scientists dominated the field. Names such as Bob Holzman, Jim Blinn, John Whitney Sr., Turner Whitted, Davis Evans, Ivan Southerland, Chuck Csuri, Ken Knowlton, and others are often cited as the earliest promoters and visionaries of CGI. In the context of simulation, motion video, and other facets of CGI, these folks are most important. However, when you read about the history of computer-generated imagery, Adobe Photoshop is never taken into account, despite the fact that more working artists use this product than any single piece of application software invented. Photoshop users are the people who illustrate millions of pages of published newspapers, magazines, and book advertisements. It allows the best of these folks to make a comfortable living while practicing their art—an unheard of situation for journeymen artists who were traditionally abused by the system. Only the big names ever got rich. Photoshop has changed the fundamentals of artistry, and this change is largely overlooked by the historians and is unknown to the public-at-large who are enriched by better art now more than ever—all thanks to Photoshop.

The folks fortunate enough to read this book can contribute to this enrichment, thanks to Bert Monroy and Adobe. I look forward to seeing the results of the next generation of art inspired by this greatest of computer tools.

—John C. Dvorak, 2002
Albany, California

Introduction

Is this a rewrite? An upgrade? I gave a lot of thought to writing this book. I lost a lot of sleep over it. I didn't even sign the contract until I was working on the last chapter.

In 1989, I co-wrote the first book on Photoshop with David Biedny. It was the only book out on Photoshop for almost two years. Later, I co-wrote two additional books with David. Nathan Moody joined the roster on one of them. I also co-authored another book with Yoshinori Kaizu that was published only in Japan.

I consider myself an artist. I love to paint. I use the word paint for lack of a better word. My medium is actually light. I have a passion for making things happen on the screen. Finding a new way of doing something and finding a new room in my imagination is what I love about the work. I would rather paint than write about it.

There is one motivating factor, though. I do have a gift that I love very much, and that is the ability to teach. When I paint, I come up with techniques that I share with my students. There is tremendous satisfaction when a student understands a concept and takes it to new heights. By sharing the techniques I have come up with, I open up peoples' minds to exploration. I thought to myself, "Why not write a book about how I do my art and reach a larger audience?" I did. It was the first book I authored by myself. Talking about my art was personal, and I felt it was something I had to do on my own.

I wrote that first book in 1998. The title was *Bert Monroy: Photorealistic Techniques with Photoshop and Illustrator*. It was published in January of 1999. It was an exciting time and the book was incredible. People sent me files they had created and thanked me for the inspiration. It felt good. Then, someone asked, "When are you going to write another one?" I hadn't thought

about writing another one. Another book? Wasn't I done? Photoshop 6 came out, and the book's content still applied. That was cool. I felt my writing days were over.

Enter Photoshop 7.

I saw version 7 early, and I got excited about it. I immediately felt the desire to help cut down peoples' learning curve and write down the stuff I found. The only problem was, as I said before, I'd rather be painting than writing. My joy of sharing won out, and I set out to write this book.

If you own my last book and thumb through this one, you might see some familiar pages. I use some of the same paintings. After all, I've only created so many. In some cases, I used the same paintings to show new techniques. In a couple of cases, I show the same techniques that I did in my other book. An example of this is the shadow of the tree in the "Cedar" painting. This painting was in the last book, but I think it is the best example of light casting shadows on angled surfaces. Not everyone bought my last book, and I felt that some of the passages in that book best explained a particular concept. For those of you who bought the first book, I added enough new content to satisfy your need for more information.

Photoshop 7 introduces some fantastic new features. These features might not be new to the world of digital imaging, but they are new to Photoshop's functionality. I remember the first time that I saw the new Brushes palette. I said, "I haven't seen anything this cool since PixelPaint." The Adobe people in the room chuckled and informed me that Jerry Harris was the guy writing the new Paint Engine. Jerry co-wrote PixelPaint with Keith MacGreggor way back when color was a new feature of the Macintosh.

Photoshop has always been a spectacular paint program; version 7 firmly establishes it as the ultimate painting tool. I look forward to seeing the kind of work people produce when they get their hands on it.

My paintings: What is my inspiration for them? The world I see. I have been asked a million times, "Why don't you just take a photograph?" This is a good question, especially when you consider that my paintings look like photographs. Well, for one thing, I'm not a photographer. To me, it is not the destination that is important; it is the journey. When I start a painting, I am filled with excitement. The incredible challenge of recreating reality is so inspiring to me.

I feel that the subjects I paint have asked to be painted. I do not go out and look for things to paint. I can be on my way to the store when a scene I want to paint suddenly jumps out in front of me.

I usually come back to a scene and sketch out the painting. I also take a few shots for reference and details. Digital cameras make this easier. I tend to carry my digital camera with me at all times to be prepared. There is no waiting for a roll to be used before I get to see the reference. In the past, I often lost the feeling to paint a scene because I waited too long for the pictures to get developed.

The still-life paintings that I do are another story. I seek these out. I look for things that pose a challenge. My still-life paintings are done from life. I set the objects next to my computer and paint what I see. I have full control over placement and lighting.

I apply the techniques I develop in the creation of these paintings to my commercial work, where deadlines prevent the luxury of experimentation. These are the same techniques that I share with you in this book. They are the essence of my artwork. My work is very personal to me. I feel the paintings, and I live them while creating them.

Because I'm sharing such a personal part of my life, let's get personal. I would like to invite you into my studio. I work at home, but technically my studio is not in my house. I like to tell people that I commute to work and that I walk there. So what if it's only about sixty-five feet away; it's still a walk.

I moved to the Bay Area in 1993. I live in Berkeley Hills. My house and studio are nestled in a Redwood grove. From my patio, there is a path that leads up to my studio.

My studio is located in a small building behind my house. A short path leads up to it past a couple of Redwood trees.

This is the side of my studio where I do my work. Many machines surround me, and they each have a function.

My main machine is a G4 dual processor with two Cinema display monitors. One screen is flat and the other is a regular tube. My main work surface is my Wacom tablet.

The interior of my studio is quiet, a far cry from growing up next to the BQE (Brooklyn-Queens Expressway) in Brooklyn, New York.

In the picture, you can see the side of the studio where I spend a major portion of my life. There are many machines around me because painting isn't the only thing that I do with computers. I also create multimedia presentations and 3D works that require a lot of computer power. It is at these terminals that I have developed many of the techniques that you learn in this book. The picture of my main machine shows the Wacom tablet that serves as my main work surface. It is a large tablet, but when you consider the amount of screen real estate that two cinema displays have, the size of the tablet makes sense.

The other side of the interior has my scanning station, printers, bookcases, and the usual stuff that goes in a studio. When I look around the studio I can't help but think how dramatically the computer has changed the way I work. In that little corner is an

airbrush workspace, a darkroom, a sculpting studio, film-editing space, a recording studio, an animation studio, my easel, and every color of paint I could ever want. All of the tools I need are there, and I never have to leave my chair.

Yes, these are exciting times we live in. May you learn much from my text. May it be an inspiration for you to unlock your imagination and have a ton of fun! Good luck! As for me, this book is finished and I can now get back to painting.

—Bert Monroy

Organization of the Book

I want to make it clear from the start that you should not consider the techniques detailed in this book as singular in purpose. The techniques that I develop in the course of creating a painting are applied to solve problems that arise in the preparation of other paintings or commercial assignments. You should look beyond the context in which these techniques are presented. You might not have to create a tree full of leaves, but the process of creating that tree can be applied to another situation.

I attempt to introduce subjects that you might not be familiar with, but that are crucial in the development of images. I introduce you to basic concepts, such as perspective and proper lighting, to give you a better understanding of how to make things work properly for a more effective illustration.

I tried to maintain a linear approach to the organization of the chapters. This gives you an idea of how I personally approach a painting. Each chapter, however, can be taken out of context to allow you to concentrate on specific techniques.

Off to a Good Start

I watch the computer graphics industry evolve with such great speed that I can't help but wonder what innovations lie just over the horizon. In Photoshop's relatively short lifespan it has developed into a tool so powerful that it is hard to imagine it can improve. However, each new version introduces new features that make you think, "How did I ever live without this?"

Before discussing the techniques, I want to introduce a few features that are new to Photoshop 7. I also want to explain some features that are referred to extensively throughout the book. Some of these features are not new, but they do require some basic knowledge for a full understanding of the techniques covered in various chapters.

File Browser

New to version 7 is the File Browser. This feature adds a new level of organization to the workflow process. It allows you to browse through files and view information. You can even open documents from within the File Browser. Yes, it opens files, though it works independently of the Open command.

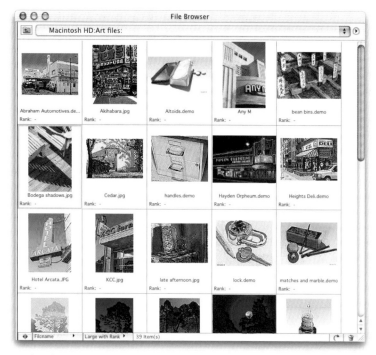

The File Browser sits on the desktop like any other window or palette in Photoshop. It can be docked into the palette well for easy access and to avoid screen clutter.

Many functions are performed with this palette that formerly required a user to exit Photoshop. Files can be moved, renamed, and even rotated. The rotation is applied to the thumbnail within the palette and is automatically applied to the file after it is opened.

Figure 1 shows the basic window displaying the contents of the currently selected folder. Clicking the toggle button on the lower left of the window expands the palette to display the information pertinent to a selected file, as shown in Figure 2. The order of viewing is selected from the categories shown in Figure 3.

1 The File Browser is similar to the contact sheets that photographers use to view the shots on a roll of film.

2 Pertinent data associated with an image can be viewed at a glance.

3 There is considerable control over the sorting of the contents of a viewed folder.

You can choose to see the details for every image at the same time (Figures 4 and 5).

As stated previously, many functions are applied in the File Browser. Figure 6 shows the drop-down menu for the palette where these functions are selected.

On the lower left of the palette, when in the extended view, there is an additional feature for viewing the details—EXIF (Figure 7). EXIF stands for Exchangeable Image File Format. This provides a look at the metadata that digital cameras embed into the image at the moment of exposure, such as F-stop, ISO ratings, and so on. It is extremely useful for those of you who need to keep track of this type of stuff. For example, I have used it to compare the data of a good shot to the data of a bad shot. This comparison gives me an idea of what I am doing wrong when I try to play photographer.

4 The details are chosen as a viewing option.

6 The drop-down menu gives you several options for altering images without having to open them.

5 The details of the images are displayed.

7 The EXIF function allows you to view the metadata attached to a file.

The File Browser was very handy in the preparation of the files for this book. I organized and eventually edited the screen grabs without exiting Photoshop, which is where the work was performed. Because the figures are named by their placement within the text, there is no way I can tell what they are until I open them. The Open dialog box does show a preview, but scrolling through 80 files is time consuming. The File Browser gives me the preview of the contents in a folder. In some cases, I need to see details of a dialog box and can see them in the preview without opening the file.

Another big time saver for me is using the File Browser open on one screen while working in Microsoft Word on another screen. This allows me to see the figures as I write a description for each of them without going back and forth between programs.

Photoshop Layers

Even though layers have been around since version 3, I feel the need to discuss their basic function. I realize many of you probably know about layers, but there are beginners who still need to understand some of the basics. Although it is not a layers book, the manual that comes with Photoshop provides a great introduction to layers. I refer to layers extensively throughout the book, as they are inevitably where the aspects of my paintings are created.

Layers are part of the image. A Photoshop document can have as many layers present in the file as memory permits. Each one of these layers can contain parts of the overall image. Layers are manipulated in as many ways as you desire without affecting the rest of the image.

Adjustment Layers

Adjustment Layers allow for economical, editable applications of valuable Photoshop commands, such as Curves, Levels, Selective Color, and Hue/Saturation. You can have multiple Adjustment Layers in a document. Even if there are layers on top that contain retouching or other major changes, the Adjustment Layer can still be changed. There is no permanent change to the base image until the job is flattened for final output.

The Clipping Group

Another cool function of layers is the Clipping Group, which is discussed a few times in the book. With this feature, one layer is used as a mask for other layers. The layers above the base image that are grouped are seen only through the active pixels of the base layer. Where there are no pixels in the base layer, the layers above the base image are invisible. The base layer, or the layer used as a mask, uses its transparency information as the mask. The diagram in Figure 8 demonstrates how it works.

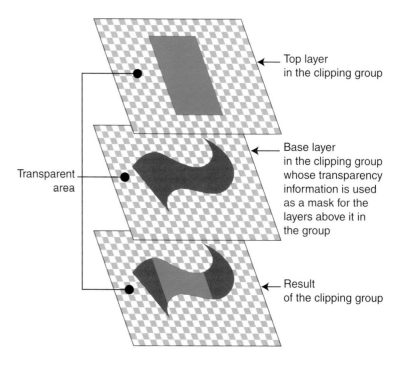

Top layer
in the clipping group

Base layer
in the clipping group
whose transparency
information is used
as a mask for the
layers above it in
the group

Transparent
area

Result
of the clipping group

8 The transparent information of the lowest layer in the group serves as a mask for the layers in the group above it.

Layer Masks

A layer mask is applied to a layer to allow portions of the layer to be seen.

In the layer mask, you apply tones from white to black with 254 additional grays in between. Where the mask is white, you can see the contents of that layer. Where the mask is black, the contents of the layer are hidden. Where the mask is gray, you see a combination of the masked layer and the layers underneath it. The lighter the gray, the more visible the masked layer. The darker the gray, the more visible are the layers underneath the masked layer.

There are other aspects of layers that will be covered throughout the book. I have placed these bits of information where they are pertinent to the topics discussed.

The Alpha Channel

Another feature that I mention many times throughout the book is the alpha channel. This feature of Photoshop is extremely important. This section gives you a brief introduction to the alpha channel and how it relates to the creation of my paintings.

The alpha channels are masks through which you can apply effects. The way they work is similar to the way a layer mask works. They both use white and black with gray tones in between. In the layer mask, the tones determine what is seen and what isn't seen. In the alpha channel, the tones expose the image to an effect. Alpha channels are basically specialized selection processes.

When you use the selection tools, you are segregating a portion of the image to be modified. The actual selection process does nothing to the image. It's the application of a filter, adjustment control, or any other modification through that selection that affects the image. This is the same concept of the alpha channel. It is merely a selection that exposes the image so that an effect can be applied.

The beauty of these alpha channels is that they can be saved and modified. When you use the Lasso, you make a selection. When you deselect, the selection is gone. If you use the Save Selection command (Select>Save Selection), the selection is sent to an alpha channel, which can be recalled as often as you want.

You can paint right in the alpha channel with any of the tools. Filters also work in the alpha channels. This opens the door to a multitude of possible effects, many of which are explored in this book.

You can use 24 channels in a Photoshop file. Some of the channels are used by the color space; for example, RGB takes up 3 channels (Red, Green, and Blue). This leaves 21 channels that can be used for alpha channels.

When you choose Save Selection, you are given the choice to send it to a new document. This sends it to a separate file that can be accessed when you choose Load Selection (Select>Load Selection) to call up an alpha channel. Saving alpha channels to a new document gives you the ability to use thousands of alpha channels.

Throughout the book, I refer to alpha channels several times. I hope you now have a basic understanding of what they are.

The Illustrator-Photoshop Connection

There are several instances throughout the book where I refer to Adobe Illustrator. I use Illustrator to create certain elements of an image. The fact that I can work on dimensionally large images that can be reduced in size without any loss of detail is very important.

Illustrator is resolution-independent. It uses vectors or mathematical information to describe the elements on a page. A rectangle has certain dimensions, color, stroke weight, and position on the page. This information is translated to an output device and conforms to the resolution of that device to produce the best possible quality print. Enlarging or reducing this information in Illustrator makes no difference. It still translates at the output stage at the best resolution of the output device.

Photoshop, on the other hand, uses pixels. It is confined to the number of pixels that the file has been assigned to its dimensions.

The number of pixels to the inch determines the size of the pixels. The higher the resolution and the smaller the pixels, the better the quality and detail of the image. When an image is enlarged, the pixels are enlarged with it, which is a risky business. If you resample upward by increasing the number of pixels to the inch, the result often looks harsh. For example, elements that should be smooth may appear jagged.

To make a long story short, I can work really big in Illustrator to ensure that I see enough detail. Later in the chapter, you will see what I mean. I start with a formula. I work in Illustrator at 400% of the actual size. I reduce the size to 25% to export it to Photoshop. Depending on the amount of detail, the numbers may change.

When Illustrator files are imported into a Photoshop file, they are rasterized—translated permanently to the resolution of the Photoshop document. The shapes are optimized to the size of the Photoshop file. Thereafter, you cannot upsize them without degradation.

For instance, if the Photoshop file is set to 72 pixels to an inch (ppi), then the imported Illustrator element will be set to 72 ppi. Illustrator does give you the capability to set resolution for its files; however, for the way I use it, this resolution setting is not necessary.

An inch is still an inch. The amount of pixels to that inch is determined by the resolution set in the Photoshop file. If the object in Illustrator measures four by six

inches, it will measure four by six inches in the Photoshop file.

If the resolution of the Photoshop file is set to 72 pixels to an inch, the element imported from Illustrator will measure 288 pixels by 432 pixels:

$$4" \times 72 \text{ ppi} = 288 \text{ pixels}$$
$$6" \times 72 \text{ ppi} = 432 \text{ pixels}$$

If the resolution of the Photoshop file is set to 300 pixels to an inch, the element imported from Illustrator then measures 1,200 pixels by 1,200 pixels by 1,800 pixels. The pixel count is simply the number of inches multiplied by the number of pixels per inch:

$$4" \times 300 \text{ ppi} = 1,200 \text{ pixels}$$
$$6" \times 300 \text{ ppi} = 1,800 \text{ pixels}$$

NOTE The color space used in both programs should match to ensure proper color transfer. If the Photoshop file is in RGB, then the Illustrator file should also be set to RGB.

There are specific details in the communication between the two programs that I suggest you reference in the manuals. In my workflow, I depend on the Copy and Paste commands to bring Illustrator elements into Photoshop. I never use the Place or Open commands to bring Illustrator files into Photoshop. This is my personal preference.

When I copy and paste Illustrator files into a Photoshop file, they are either pixels or paths. I import them as pixels if I already assigned the desired attributes to shapes

created in Illustrator. In the course of the book, I demonstrate several times when I do this and the reasons why.

There are also times when I import the Illustrator files as paths. When they enter the Photoshop file, they appear in the Paths palette. The imported paths become a Work Path. The Work Path is a temporary path, and it is necessary to save the path if you want to use it more than once. If I import Illustrator files as paths, it is because I intend to assign color, texture, and any other desired attribute in Photoshop. Paths become a method for selecting areas for colorization and so on.

In the Beginning...

Here I sit in front of a blank screen, ready to begin. There is a feeling of anticipation that was lacking when I sat before a blank canvas. The possibilities are so much greater in the digital world. The mere fact that I can select a color immediately lets the creative flow take me wherever I want to go. There is no time wasted mixing colors to get just that perfect blue for the sky.

The process for creating an image varies based on what I intend to accomplish. The computer makes it very easy for the artist to wear many hats. The computer makes it possible to work as a sculptor, photographer, painter, video and film editor, sound producer, special effects artist, and it makes it possible to access so many additional graphic arts skills—all without having to leave your chair.

Where do I start?

Usually an image starts out as a sketch. This is a series of paths created using the Pen tool to form the basic shapes of the elements in the painting. At times, the sketch is a pencil drawing that is then scanned into the computer. It can also be outlined in the computer from the start. Basically, the process is identical to sketching on canvas with a pencil or charcoal prior to the application of the paint.

The Sketch

In Figure 9, you see the paths laid out for the "late afternoon" image, which is on the cover. It is a series of simple lines, laid out with the Pen tool.

These various paths are later separated into individual paths that are used to make selections during the rendering of the image. In layers, these selections are filled with colors to form the elements of an image. Figure 10 shows the paths for the blinds, which are visible in the reflection in the mirror and are separated and ready to be made into a selection.

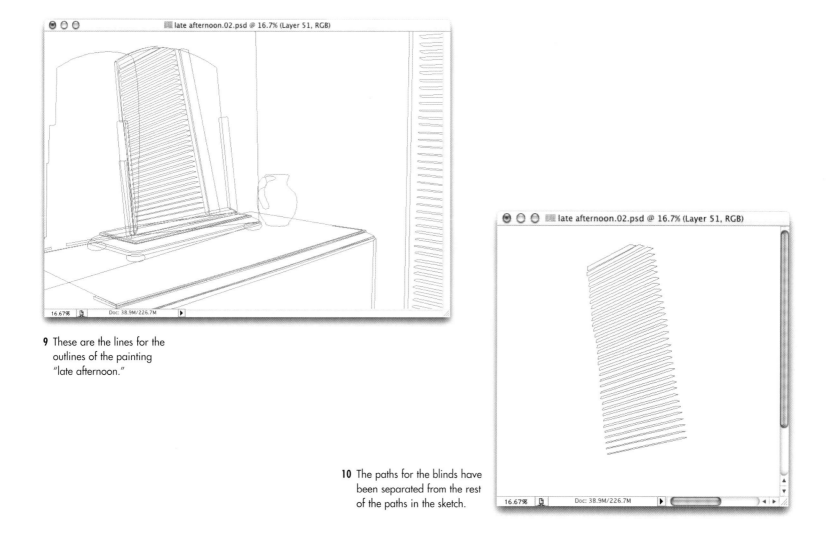

9 These are the lines for the outlines of the painting "late afternoon."

10 The paths for the blinds have been separated from the rest of the paths in the sketch.

Walking a Thin Line

As mentioned previously, I often use Illustrator for certain parts of an image. The image "Akihabara," seen in the Gallery, has a couple of bicycles in the foreground. The spokes of the bicycle tires are very thin. The Line tool in Photoshop is limited to a single pixel in width. This is thin enough for most cases, but in this painting, it is too thick (Figure 11). Take into account the anti-aliasing to make the spokes look smooth, and they get even thicker.

Remember how Photoshop rasterizes the incoming Illustrator file? In Illustrator, I created the spokes and stroked them with a mere .24-point stroke. This is a very thin line. When it is brought into Photoshop, the result is a line that is much thinner than what I could have achieved using the Line tool (Figure 12).

11 The tire spokes on the bike are thinner than what could have been created in Photoshop.

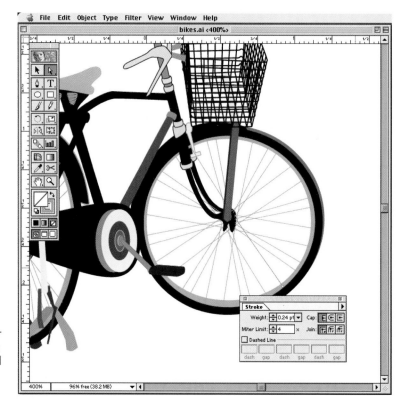

12 The tire spokes are created in Illustrator using a .24-point stroke, and then they are brought into Photoshop.

Realistic Text

The rasterization process comes in handy on other occasions. The menus in the painting "Solano Grill" have tiny text visible on them. To get the effect of text this small in Photoshop is a trial-and-error process, not to mention time consuming. Creating actual text in Illustrator and

rasterizing it into Photoshop is simple and achieves higher quality (Figures 13 and 14.) The menu on the left has the imported text. The other two menus are first altered a bit.

For reference, I went to the restaurant and got one of their take-out menus and

copied it. Of course it seems a bit extreme to actually retype the entire menu; however, this is one of my fine art pieces, and I never use scans in my fine art. There is no law that states you cannot use a scan. I am just trying to show you my process.

SOUPS

Seafood Chowder with Manila Clams, Prawns & Scallions
Cup: $3.25 Bowl: $5.25

Soup du Jour
A. Q.

HOUSE SALADS

Organic Garden Salad with Caramelized Walnuts, Grapefruit Segments,
Cucumbers, & Cherry Tomatoes served with a Citrus & Herb Vinaigrette
$5.25

Classic Caesar Salad with Crisp Whole Leaf Romaine Lettuce,
Salted Anchovies, Herbed Croutons, & Freshly Grated Asiago Cheese
$5.25

Combination Soup & Salad
Half Order of Selected House Salad with a Cup of Seafood Chowder
$5.95

SPECIALTY SALADS

Warm Spinach & Pear Salad with Sun Dried Cranberries, Cucumbers
Caramalized Shallots, Cherry Tomatoes, Chopped Bacon
and served with a Citrus & Herb Vinaigrette
$6.95

Grilled Prawns and Papaya Salad with Field Greens & Cherry Tomatoes
and served with a Tangy Mint Vinaigrette
$7.75

Granny Smith Apple & Chicken Salad in an Iceberg Lettuce Cup
served with a Toasted Walnut and Yogurt Dressing
$7.75

Specialty Soup & Salad Combination
Half Order of Selected Specialty Salad with a Cup of Soup
$7.75

GOURMET SANDWICHES

Marinated Chicken Breast Sandwich
on Sourdough Slices with Spinach and Tomatoes, Pepperoncini, Applewood Smoked Bacon
$7.25

Grilled Black Angus Rib Eye Steak Sandwich
on a French Deli Roll with Caramalized Onions and Teriyaki Glaze
$9.95

rganic Garden Salad with Caramelized Walnuts, Grapefruit Segments,
Cucumbers, & Cherry Tomatoes served with a Citrus & Herb Vinaigrette
$5.25

Classic Caesar Salad with Crisp Whole Leaf Romaine Lettuce,
Salted Anchovies, Herbed Croutons, & Freshly Grated Asiago Cheese
$5.25

Combination Soup & Salad
Half Order of Selected House Salad with a Cup of Seafood Chowder
$5.95

arm Spinach & Pear Salad with Sun Dried Cranberries, Cucumbers
Caramalized Shallots, Cherry Tomatoes, Chopped Bacon
and served with a Citrus & Herb Vinaigrette
$6.95

Grilled Prawns and Papaya Salad with Field Greens & Cherry Tomatoes
and served with a Tangy Mint Vinaigrette
$7.75

SEAFOOD, PASTA, AND GRILLS

Warm Spinach & Pear Salad with Sun Dried Cranberries, Cucumbers
Caramalized Shallots, Cherry Tomatoes, Chopped Bacon
and served with a Citrus & Herb Vinaigrette
$6.95

Grilled Prawns and Papaya Salad with Field Greens & Cherry Tomatoes
and served with a Tangy Mint Vinaigrette
$7.75

Granny Smith Apple & Chicken Salad in an Iceberg Lettuce Cup
served with a Toasted Walnut and Yogurt Dressing
$7.75

Specialty Soup & Salad Combination
Half Order of Selected Specialty Salad with a Cup of Soup
$7.75

13 The text of the menu from the Illustrator file.

14 The text of the menus in the Photoshop file.

Tiny Details

There are times when adding tiny details adds a little fun to the image. Figure 15 is an image called "Future City." I created it in 1992 using Photoshop 2.0. There were no layers then, but the Illustrator-Photoshop connection was there. The close-up in Figure 15, of the window on the lower right of the painting, shows a man at work at his desk. The CDs on his desk, reproduced in Figure 16, have titles on them.

You may accuse me of being excessively detail-oriented, not to mention sick, to take the time to put titles that nobody could possibly read on these tiny CDs. This is not true. A detail-obsessed, sick person would have made sure the perspective on the type was better.

15 The image *Future City* was created with Photoshop 2.0 in 1992. The window on the lower-right corner of the image shows a man sitting at a desk.

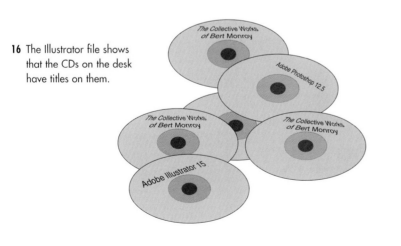

16 The Illustrator file shows that the CDs on the desk have titles on them.

Creating a Chain with a Pattern Brush

There are other features available in Illustrator, which makes it the ideal place to create certain elements for an image. Figure 17 shows a detail from "Rendez-vous," a painting that is highlighted later in the book. Note the chain that connects the sign to its bracket.

Normally, I am inclined to paint each of these links. Or, perhaps I would create one link and duplicate it several times, and then rotate each duplicate into position on the chain. This is the way I used to tackle this sort of problem. Version 8 of Illustrator changed this. Keep in mind that Illustrator is now up to version 10.

Illustrator's Pattern Brush works differently than what one might associate with a typical pattern.

Using Illustrator, the basic link was created by making an elliptical shape with the Pen (Figure 18). The path was stroked with a line weight heavy enough to represent a link in the chain.

With the Scissors tool, the ellipse was cut at each of the four points—on the top, the bottom, and on both sides.

17 This is a detail of the painting "Rendez-vous." Notice the chain on the side of the sidewalk sign. It was created with the new Pattern Brush in Illustrator.

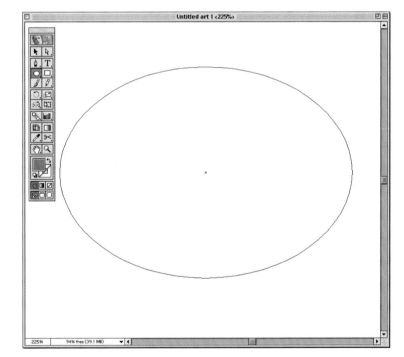

18 An ellipse was created in Illustrator.

This created four, separate curved lines. The path was then outlined (Object>Path>Outline Stroke). This made four distinct sections of a single chain link that were then filled with a brown color. Although they appear separated from each other in Figure 19, the pieces were in fact not separated. I did this for the book only, so that you can see the four distinct pieces.

The two shapes on the left were cloned and moved over to the right to form an interlocking effect with the original piece of chain. They were then filled with a light brown color (Figure 20).

I then copied the two light brown curved sections on a vertical axis with the Reflect tool. I used the center of the original link as the point for the Reflect axis, as shown in Figure 21.

The two top sections of the original link were selected and brought to the front, as shown in Figure 22. This created the illusion of interlocking chain links.

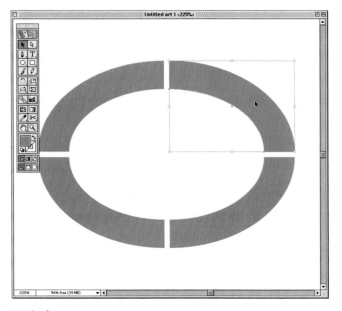

19 The four separate shapes created from the original ellipse.

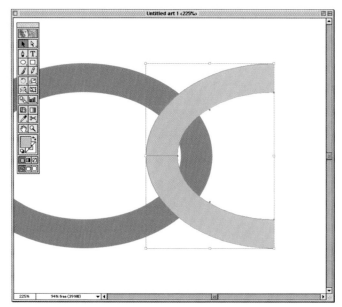

20 The two curved sections on the left were cloned and moved to interlock with the original link. They were then filled with a light brown color.

21 The two curved sections were reflected on a vertical axis to interlock with the left side of the original link.

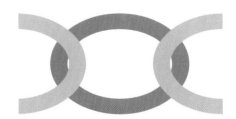

22 The two curved sections on the top of the original link were brought to the front to complete the look of a chain link.

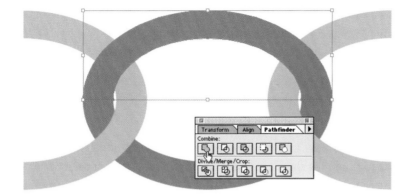

23 The two curved sections were joined to form a single section.

Just for the sake of cleanliness, using the Pathfinder option, I joined the sections for the top of the original link into a single section (Figure 23). The same was done to the two lower sections of the link.

The sections that made up the side links had to remain as separate sections because their positions were required to remain intact to create the three-dimensional effect of a chain link. One appeared in front of the center link while the other was placed in the back.

Next, it was necessary to create the path for the chain that would eventually be made with the link that I just created in Illustrator (Figure 24). Switching to Photoshop, I used the Path tool to create the path for the chain. I copied this path to the Clipboard.

In Illustrator, the path for the chain is pasted into the document where the link had already been created (Figure 25).

24 In Photoshop, I used the Pen tool to create a path for the chain. This path was then copied over to Illustrator.

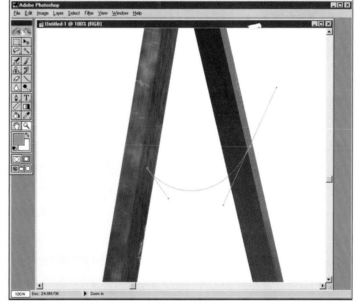

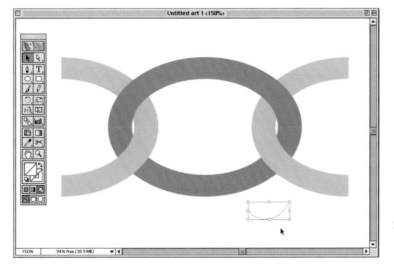

25 The path for the chain is pasted into the Illustrator file with the link.

Obviously, the link was very large. Using the Scale tool, I reduced the link to a size that was adequate for the chain (Figure 26).

The entire link was selected and New Pattern Brush was chosen from the Brush palette. In the dialog box that popped up, I chose New Pattern Brush (Figure 27).

After the brush type is selected, a second dialog box appears where you can enter parameters for the brush. I left the default settings and named the brush Chain link, as shown in Figure 28.

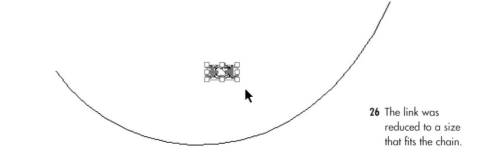

26 The link was reduced to a size that fits the chain.

27 The entire link was selected and New Pattern Brush was chosen from the Brushes palette. In the dialog box, I chose Pattern for the brush type.

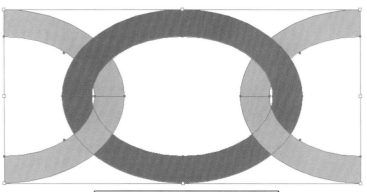

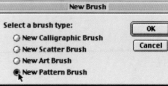

28 I named the brush Chain link in the second dialog box that is associated with the creation of a new brush. I used the default settings.

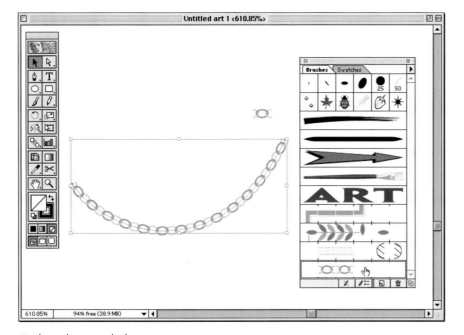

29 The path was stroked with the pattern of the chain link.

The newly created pattern brush then appeared in the Brushes palette. I selected the path for the chain and clicked on the pattern brush in the palette. This automatically applied the pattern to the currently selected path, as shown in Figure 29. The path was then transformed into a chain.

This completed chain was copied to the Clipboard and sent over to Photoshop for inclusion in the painting, as shown in Figure 30.

30 The path with the chain link was copied to the Clipboard and copied over to Photoshop.

Spring into Action with Transform Again

Certain path controls that are not available in Photoshop do exist in Illustrator. Transform Again is one of them. The image, "the gate," was created on location with a PowerBook (Figure 31). I spent five days sitting at the site creating the paths for the image in Illustrator. I spent four evenings turning those paths into selections in Photoshop, so that they could be filled with the appropriate colors.

Certain parts of the painting were created entirely in Illustrator with simple shading added in Photoshop. This is one of those circumstances when the tools in Illustrator do things to paths that can't be done in Photoshop. The spring visible on the side of the gate is an example (Figure 32).

The spring on the gate started out as a small circle in Illustrator (Figure 33). The circle was then filled with a beige color.

31 The image, "the gate," was created on location with a PowerBook.

32 The spring on the gate was created in Illustrator.

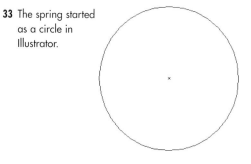

33 The spring started as a circle in Illustrator.

I duplicated the circle on a vertical axis with the Reflect tool (Shift-Option-drag can also be used), as shown in Figure 34. A rectangle connected the two circles (Figure 35). The three objects were then turned into a single object with the Unite/Pathfinder function, as shown in Figure 36.

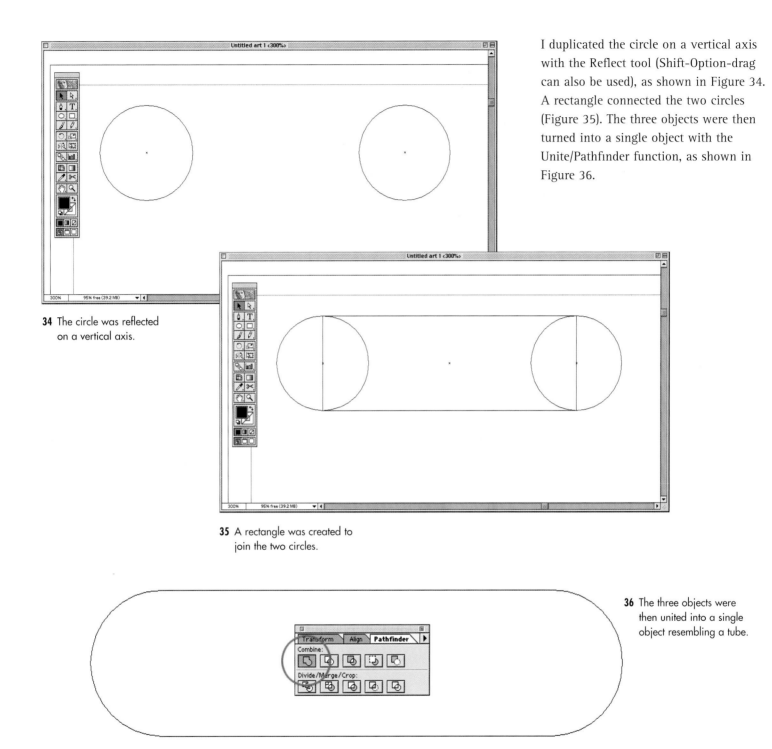

34 The circle was reflected on a vertical axis.

35 A rectangle was created to join the two circles.

36 The three objects were then united into a single object resembling a tube.

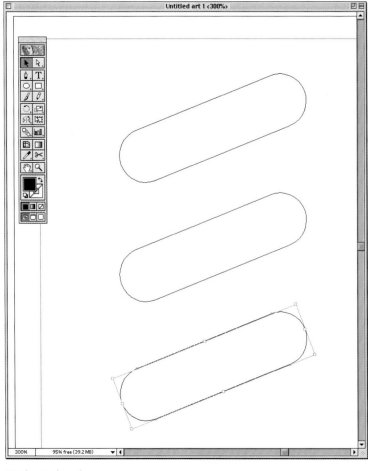

37 The single coil was duplicated multiple times to form the entire length of the spring.

With the Rotate tool, I angled the tube. I cloned the tube directly below the original. Pressing Command-D (Control-D on the PC), which is Transform Again, the clone was duplicated again and again, until the entire length of the spring was created (Figure 37).

I selected the objects, and using the Reflect tool, I made a copy that was flipped on a vertical axis.

This new set was filled with black and sent to the back of the original spring sections. This new set served as the back part of the spring, visible through the coils in front, as shown in Figure 38.

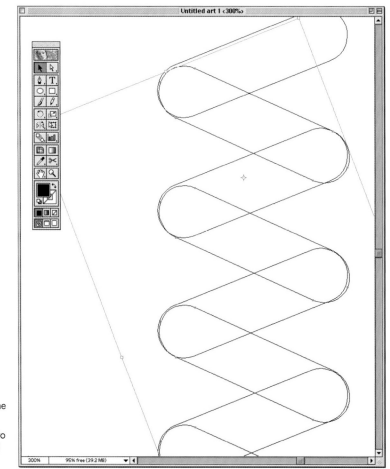

38 The coils representing the front of the spring are duplicated and flipped to form the rear portion of the spring.

The additional hardware was created at the top and bottom of the coils, as shown in Figure 39. The various objects were filled with colors chosen to represent the metal and the different angles for the reflections of light.

The finished spring was then imported into Photoshop. There, it was rotated to the angle needed for placement within the scene (Figure 40). The Dodge and Burn tools were used to add shadows and highlights to the spring, as shown in Figure 41. The tools were used in their default state, which was sufficient for creating the highlights and shadows needed for dimensionality.

39 The additional hardware of the spring was added to the top and bottom.

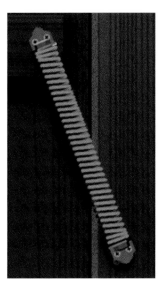

40 The spring was imported into Photoshop and rotated into position.

41 The Dodge and Burn tools were used to add shadows and highlights.

The House Blend

Another feature in Illustrator that I often use is the Blend tool. This tool allows you to take two totally different paths and make a blend or metamorphosis between them. This saves a tremendous amount of time in calculating and preparing the shapes needed for certain parts of an image. Take the cover image again—zooming in on the reflection in the mirror, you see the tiny holes in the blinds through which the lift strings penetrate the slats (Figure 42). In Figure 43, you see the paths used to create those tiny holes.

The basic shape for the top hole was created in Illustrator. A second path for the hole further down the blinds was also created. Perspective was taken into account to achieve realism. You are looking up at the top hole while the one further down is closer to your eye level. The angle for the holes shifts as they travel down the course of the blinds conforming to the viewer's point of view. Figure 44 shows the two different angled views in an Illustrator document.

NOTE For the sake of demonstration, the two paths were placed much closer than the actual paths appearing in the painting.

With the two paths selected, the Blend tool is chosen. Double-clicking on it pops up a dialog box where you can set attributes for how the tool will respond (Figure 45).

42 A close look at the reflection in the mirror reveals the tiny holes in the slats of the blinds.

43 The holes in the slats were first created as paths.

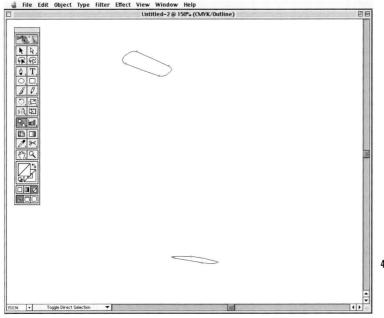

Setting the Spacing to Specified Steps allows you to set the number of iterations that are created. Clicking on one point in the first object, then clicking on the corresponding point in the second object produces the interpolated steps in between. Figure 46 shows the result of the blend between the two paths that are used for the holes in the blinds. The final paths were exported to Photoshop where they were used to make selections for the final application of color.

44 Two paths were created to represent the top hole and the bottom, and each had angles to simulate the perspective view.

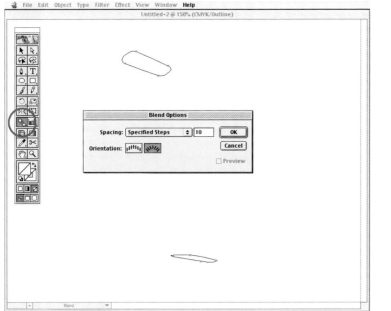

45 The dialog box for the Blend tool in Illustrator.

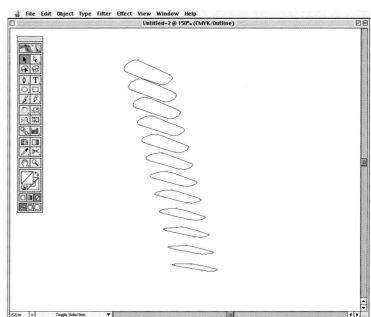

46 The result of the Blend tool applied to the two paths.

Perspective

The final subject I want to touch on in this chapter is perspective. Perspective is very important in the beginning stages of an image. Proper perspective adds dimension to an image. Shading completes this task, but that is covered in a later chapter.

Perspective follows certain rules in nature. Any deviation from these rules will make your image look unrealistic. There are times when you can bend these rules. This produces effects of exaggerated views such as a worm's eye view or a bird's eye view.

It is important to have a basic understanding of how perspective works. In my last book, I dedicated an entire chapter to perspective, but in this book I simplify it a bit.

Adding the effect of a third dimension gives the viewer a sense of movement within the scene. It can also add an element of excitement to an otherwise simple image. Perspective allows us to portray the complex, three-dimensional world we inhabit within a two-dimensional plane and make it believable.

When I first approach a subject to paint, I deliberately study it from exaggerated angles. These angles serve many purposes, depending on what I am trying to emphasize.

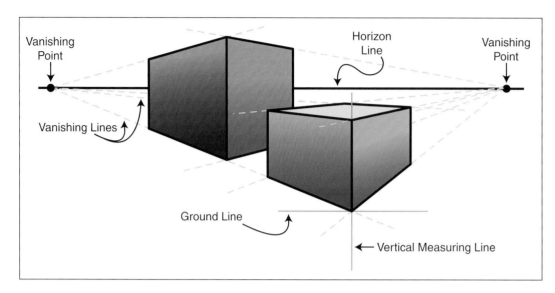

47 The rules of perspective.

Exaggerated perspective is also used to solve certain problems that might arise in the preparation of an illustration. Getting a worm's eye view, for example, can be achieved by using a strong perspective, one that has the vanishing point at the apex of the observer's point of view.

To understand the process of creating images with proper perspective, it is crucial to understand how perspective works. There are certain fundamental principles at work that create formulas to achieve proper perspective (Figure 47).

Fundamental Terms of Perspective

To understand the process of creating images with proper perspective, it is crucial to understand certain fundamental terms:

- Horizon
- Vertical measuring line
- Horizon line
- Ground line
- Vanishing points
- Vanishing lines

Horizon

All the elements within an image are created from the point of view of the person looking at the image. The horizon is the eye level of the person viewing the scene. When you place the horizon below the ground line, you get a worm's eye view. When you place the horizon near the center, you get a normal view. When you place the horizon above the ground line, you get a bird's eye view.

Vertical Measuring Line

The vertical measuring line is an imaginary line drawn from the bottom to the top of the objects that appear in the scene. This vertical measuring line determines the height of an object.

Horizon Line

The horizon line is basically the plane at which the land and sky meet off in the distance. The horizon line is always a straight line, even though the Earth is round. Establishing this horizon line is crucial, even if buildings, hills, or other elements in the image obscure it.

Ground Line

The ground line, also referred to as the ground plane, is the bottom of an object being rendered or the place where it touches the ground.

Vanishing Points

Vanishing points are the points on the horizon where parallel vanishing lines converge.

Vanishing Lines

Vanishing lines are the horizontal lines of an object that converge at the vanishing points.

Figure 47 is a diagram that displays these various functions at work. Notice that the relationship between the two boxes and their environment is effective in creating the illusion of spatial reality.

Putting Things into Perspective

Neither Illustrator nor Photoshop have the capability to render three-dimensional objects. Both are 2D drawing and imaging programs. There are many 3D programs available on the market. If 3D is necessary, and you have the time to create and render such an image, choosing one of these packages will solve many of your problems. In Illustrator and Photoshop, however, it is sometimes necessary to emulate a third dimension in two-dimensional space.

To achieve this sense of three-dimensional space you must follow the rules set forth earlier. The vanishing points may lie far beyond the boundaries of the Photoshop image. Making the canvas size large enough to display the vanishing points might make the file size huge. This is a very good time to use Illustrator. Illustrator has a drawing board large enough to accommodate vanishing points as far from each other as necessary without eating up RAM or disc space, as Photoshop would do.

In Illustrator, I start up a new file. In it, I draw a box that has the dimensions of what the final Photoshop image will be. I also establish the horizon line and a few lines to serve as vertical measuring lines (Figure 48).

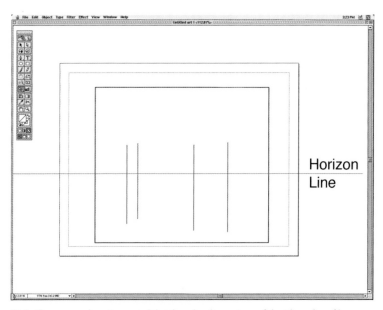

48 In Illustrator, a box is created that has the dimensions of the Photoshop file.

Vanishing lines are generated that converge on the established vanishing point (Figure 49). Over these vanishing lines I create lines that fit within the boundaries of the Photoshop file. I create one for the top and one for the bottom, as seen in Figure 50. Using the Blend tool, described earlier in this chapter, interim steps are generated. These resulting lines are imported into the Photoshop file where they are used as guides for elements in the image (Figure 51).

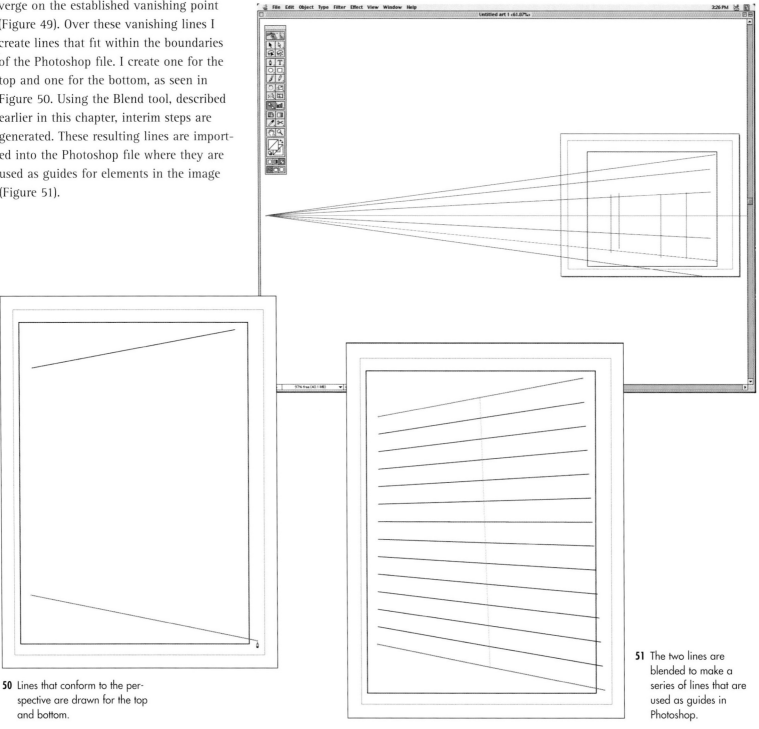

49 The vanishing lines are established.

50 Lines that conform to the perspective are drawn for the top and bottom.

51 The two lines are blended to make a series of lines that are used as guides in Photoshop.

The Art of Brush Making

The ability to create custom brushes has been around for quite some time now. In the days when traditional paints and brushes were used, I customized my brushes by shaving them into different shapes. Now, digital custom brushes give you the power to define your own shapes and how those shapes are applied when you paint.

Photoshop 7 introduced what is, in my opinion, one of the most exciting features to come along in quite some time—the capability to create Brush Presets. These are not your ordinary, everyday, run-of-the-mill brushes; these tools perform tricks. In previous versions of Photoshop, I created dense foliage by clicking with a brush the shape of a single leaf or leaf cluster (for what seemed like an eternity). A single stroke now creates an entire forest of trees.

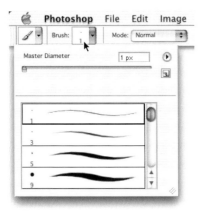

1 Brushes can still be accessed via the tool bar below the menu.

You could always make new brushes, but Photoshop 7 introduces an avalanche of ways to modify them—for color, for spacing, for texture, for randomness. Each brush can now have an infinite number of subtle variations, and all can be saved for later use. In this chapter we will be studying the extraordinarily flexible Brush Attributes feature in the Brushes palette, and discussing some practical uses for all that power.

2 Looking under the Windows menu we find a new window choice— **Brushes**. This is the heart of the new Paint Engine in Photoshop 7.

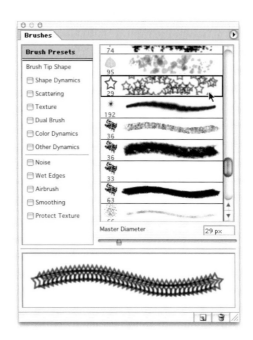

3 In the Brushes palette you are presented with a list of available Brush Presets. These are presets that come bundled with the program or they are presets that you have created.

One of the most valuable features in this window is the preview area at the bottom. Any attributes assigned to a brush are shown in the preview, making it very easy to create brushes that behave the way you intend them to behave. The only drawback is that color controls can't be viewed.

4 The drop-down menu allows you to customize the way you view the available brushes. This is also where you save, delete, rename, and load brushes. There is also a section at the bottom of the menu, starting with Assorted Brushes, where you can quickly load presets that perform specific functions.

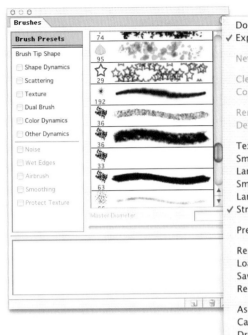

5 The second choice of controls within the Brushes palette deals with the basic Tip controls. These controls were formerly found in the tool bar. You can choose a particular brush shape. I have chosen the star-shaped brush to demonstrate some of the next few features.

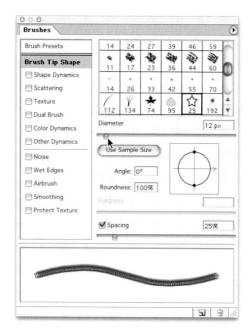

6 The first control in the **Brush Tip Shape** window is the setting for the **Diameter** of the brush. This is the only control that is available in the tool bar, as seen in Figure 1. The open and close Bracket keys, on the keyboard, also control the diameter.

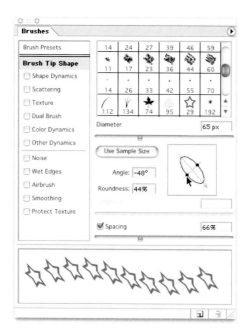

7 The **Use Sample Size** button appears if you have a Custom Brush shape selected. It becomes active if you have modified the size of that Custom Brush. Pressing the button will restore it to the original brush size. At other times the button is not visible.

You can adjust the **Angle** and **Roundness** of the brush either numerically or visually. Notice that the adjustment I have made is reflected in the preview box.

The **Hardness** is also controlled in this window. This is the control for the edge of the brush tip. A setting of zero will produce a soft-edged or blurred brush. A setting of 100% will produce a hard-edged or shape-looking brush tip. The particular brush I have selected can't be modified with Hardness, so the control is inactive.

The **Spacing** controls the amount of space that falls between the brush shapes as the brush is stroked across the canvas. A high percentage will produce a dotted line effect. The minimum percentage (1%) will produce a solid line.

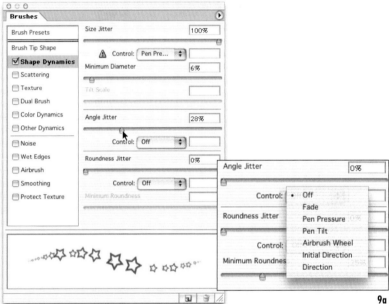

8 **Shape Dynamics** is where this new feature starts to take off. The **Size Jitter** allows you to make the brush randomize the diameter of the brush tip as the tool is stroked across the canvas.

Figure 8a shows the Control settings. They can be set to respond to a stylus. My Wacom tablet takes full advantage of these settings.

The **Minimum Diameter** allows you to set a limit to the smallest size a brush tip can be.

9 The **Angle Jitter** allows you to randomize the angle of the brush tip. In the preview of this figure, you will notice that the stars have different angles. Compare the two larger stars in the center of the preview to the same two stars in the preview of Figure 8.

Figure 9b shows the controls for the Angle Jitter. Later in this chapter, you will see how I have used these controls to create the stitching on cloth that is visible in the painting on the cover of this book.

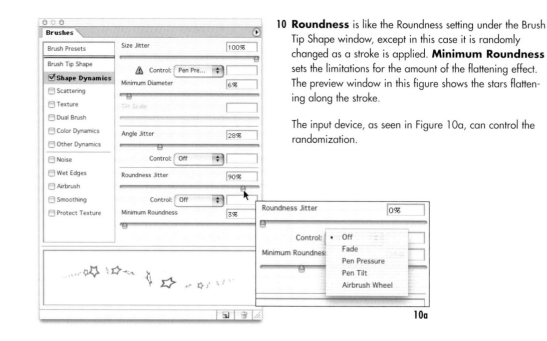

10 Roundness is like the Roundness setting under the Brush Tip Shape window, except in this case it is randomly changed as a stroke is applied. **Minimum Roundness** sets the limitations for the amount of the flattening effect. The preview window in this figure shows the stars flattening along the stroke.

The input device, as seen in Figure 10a, can control the randomization.

10a

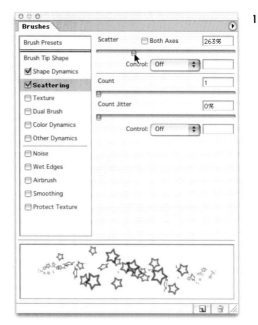

11 Scattering distributes the brush tips away from the actual stroke being applied to the canvas. The higher the percentage, the further they will travel.

The scatter is applied up and down from where the stroke is drawn. The scatter can be applied to both axes, which will cause the tips to be applied left and right as well as above and below. This is controlled by the input device.

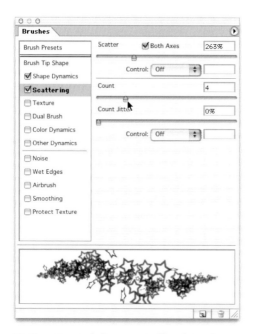

12 Count controls the amount of brush tips that are generated. A high number will make a dense brush stroke. If the Count is left at 0, the stroke will use the current Spacing parameters set in the Brush Tip Shape window. This is controlled by the input device.

13 Count Jitter randomizes the Count amount along the stroke as it is applied over the canvas. This is controlled by the input device.

14 Texture applies a user-defined texture to the stroke. From this point on I have changed brush tip from the star to a large, circular-shaped brush.

15 Scale controls the size of the texture within the stroke. The **Depth** controls the strength of the pattern over the stroke. The higher the percentage, the more the texture will be seen. A low percentage will allow the original brush shape to show through.

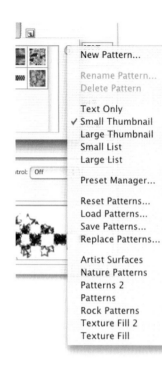

16 The texture choices are the patterns that are currently available with the program. You can open saved patterns the same way you can within the Pattern controls. Figure 16a shows the menu of the Texture Chooser where you can customize the settings. You will notice that there are some groupings available at the bottom of the menu for quick access to often-used textures.

16a

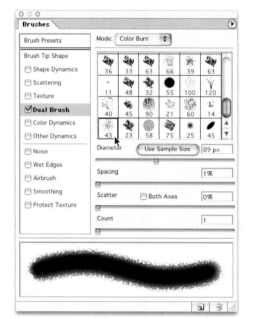

18a

17 The **Texture Each Tip** option makes the **Minimum Depth** and **Depth Jitter** controls active. This control adds the randomization to the application of the texture over the stroke as it is applied to the canvas.

18 Dual Brush uses a second brush to create an effect over the currently selected brush tip. The second brush is randomly rotated over the main brush. The effect is controlled by the **Mode** that is applied to the dual brush (Figure 18a).

20 **Color Dynamics** is a useful section, but it lacks a color preview for the settings. You will see further in this chapter that these controls are extremely useful.

The **Foreground/Background Jitter** switches between the colors that are currently selected in the Toolbox. The higher the percentage, the stronger the saturation of the Background color that is visible in the stroke.

Hue Jitter introduces other colors to the stroke, much like the Add Noise filter introduces colors to the noise if Monochromatic is not selected.

Saturation Jitter randomizes the amount of saturation the colors will have along the stroke.

Brightness Jitter randomizes the amount of brightness the colors will have along the stroke. Some of the brush tips will be darker or lighter than they would be if this option was not selected.

19 The controls at the bottom of the Dual Brush window are the same as the controls found elsewhere for the main brush. Modifying these settings will affect the dual brush's effect over the main brush as the main brush is stroked over the canvas.

21 **Purity** shifts the colors toward or away from the neutral axis. Figure 21 has four strokes created with the Pattern Stamp tool. The top stroke is made with a multi-colored pattern. The second stroke is the same tool, with the same pattern in Impressionist mode. The third stroke has the Purity pushed to 100%. The fourth stroke has the Purity lowered to –100%.

22 **Other Dynamics** sets a jitter for Opacity and Flow. The **Opacity** is the level of translucency of the brush stroke, allowing layers beneath it to show through. The **Flow** is the amount of paint being applied. Jittering will randomize these effects as the stroke is applied across the canvas. Figure 22a has the Opacity Jitter set to 100%. Figure 22b has the Flow Jitter set to 100%. Figure 22c has both the Opacity and the Flow Jitter set to 100%.

22a

22b

The bottom section of the controls are not adjustable.

22c

24 **Wet Edges** lightens the central portion of the stroke, creating the effect of paint buildup at the outer edges.

Airbrush simulates the airbrush-style buildup to a stroke. If the brush is held in one position the paint will be applied slowly as if building up the amount of paint.

Smoothing—If you create a free-hand stroke across the canvas, this feature eliminates any hard edges or bumps added to the stroke as a result of a shaky hand.

Protect Texture—If you have chosen a pattern or texture for the overall image, any brush chosen conforms to that texture. If a particular Brush Preset is chosen that has its own texture, that texture will be overridden by the texture applied to the image.

23 **Noise** applies noise to the stroke. Unfortunately the amount of noise can't be adjusted.

Putting the Brushes to Work

The "late afternoon" image (Figure 25) was the first painting I created in Photoshop 7. My customized brush presets proved very useful, by saving time and by creating the realistic effects that I was looking for.

25 The "late afternoon" painting was the first painting I created with Photoshop 7.

As I discussed previously, creating foliage is one process that utilizes the new brushes to make your life easier. In Figure 26, you see a close-up of the reflection of the window in the mirror. Note the darker green trees visible in the distance. These trees are created with a single stroke of a brush preset.

I decided to make the trees look like maple trees. With the Pen tool, I created the basic shape of a single maple leaf (Figure 27). It is important to set the Pen tool to Paths and not Shape Layer (see manual). In a separate layer, the path was filled with black. Other colors might not make the brush opaque enough.

NOTE   Hues other than black might be useful in situations when it is necessary to make the stroke transparent.

26 Trees are visible in the reflection in the mirror. The smaller, darker trees in the background were created with a brush preset.

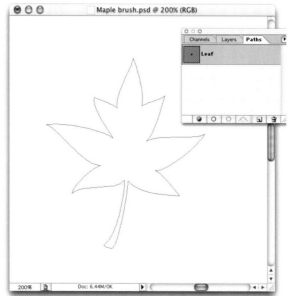

27 With the Pen tool, a path is created in the shape of a maple leaf.

28a Define Brush is chosen from the Edit menu to save the brush shape in the Brushes palette.

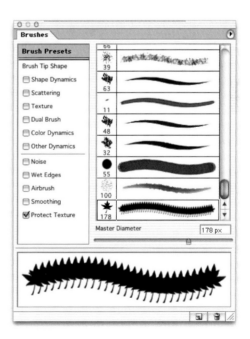

29 The new Brushes palette is where you can add multiple functions to a single brush.

28b When a new brush is created, a dialog box pops up that allows you to name the brush.

The black leaf was then selected with the Rectangular Marquee tool. The Eye icon for the Background layer was turned off. This was necessary to make the area around the leaf transparent. If the Background layer were turned on, the brush would have white behind the brush shape. To create the brush, Define Brush was chosen from the Edit menu (Figure 28a). A dialog box appears that allows you to name the brush (Figure 28b).

The customized brush shape automatically appears in the Brushes palette at the bottom of the list. With the leaf brush selected, I went into the Brushes palette. This is where the magic begins (Figure 29)!

Selecting one of the tools in the Toolbox that utilizes brush shapes activates the functions in the Brushes window. Selecting your newly created brush shape will make it appear in the preview box. You will notice that the look of the brush, as it is passed along a stroke, appears in the preview. At first, the stroke is a series of leaves running along the stroke. I wanted to recreate the randomness of the leaf shapes found along the branches of a tree. In reality, the leaves on a tree are the same shape with slight variations in shapes and sizes. The extreme randomness is the result of the viewing angle. Two identical leaves appear different on a 2D plane as a result of the variation with which they fall in your viewpoint. To illustrate this point, Figure 30 shows the same leaf viewed from two different angles. Performing a non-uniform scale (Edit> Transform>Scale) on the leaf shown on the right—making it thinner—creates the illusion of foreshortening or angled view.

NOTE The example shown in Figure 30 is to demonstrate a point and is not part of the brush-making process.

The first thing I needed to do was to separate the leaves from each other in the preview area of the palette to make it easier to see the modifications I was going to make to the brush stroke. At the same time, this also created the fullness of the leaves on the tree. The Scattering section of the palette allows you to play with these controls. Scattering distributed leaves outside or away from the actual stroke (Figure 31). The higher the number, the further the distance they spread. Selecting Both Axes ensures an equal distribution on both sides of the stroke. I set the number to 450%. Keep in mind that these settings worked in this particular instance. One of the advantages of having the preview area is that you can see the results of the settings you choose.

The Count setting lets you increase the number of leaves generated as the stroke is applied. I set the Count to 4. The Count Jitter sets randomness to the count as it is being generated. The Count Jitter was set to 98%. These were the settings I saw fit for what I was creating at the time; they do not signify a formula of any kind. When you make modifications to customized brushes, settings are determined based on what you see in the preview window.

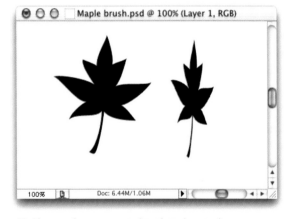

30 This graphic was created in Photoshop to show you two leaves with identical structure that appear to be viewed at different angles as a result of foreshortening in 3D space when the leaves are resized with different horizontal and vertical scalings.

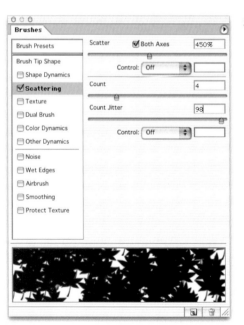

31 The Scattering portion of the Brushes palette lets you set a *distribution for the brush shape at angles at a distance from the actual stroke.*

Keep in mind that Photoshop is not a 3D program; thus, any foreshortening caused by depth perception is actually being simulated on a 2D plane. Foreshortening was achieved by playing with the settings under the Shape Dynamics portion of the palette (Figure 32). I increased the Size Jitter so that the brush would change the size of the leaves with the greatest variety, as it was dragged across the canvas. I set the Minimum Diameter to 15%. Lower settings for the brush create leaves that are too small. A leaf as small as 1% of its final size does not appear as a leaf, but rather a clump about to open as a leaf.

I set the Angle Jitter to 100% so that the leaves appear at totally random angles as the stroke travels across the canvas. The Control for both of these settings was set to Pen Pressure. When doing this, the effects were subject to the pressure applied to the stylus on my Wacom tablet as the brush was passed across the canvas.

The Roundness Jitter was where I got the effect of foreshortening. This dramatically altered the shapes of the leaves, giving the illusion of viewing some of them from the side. I increased the Roundness Jitter to 90%, and then I set the Minimum Roundness

to 15%. A lower setting has the effect of flattening the leaf shape so that it appears to be a flat line, which is distracting and unrealistic.

Next, I wanted the individual leaves to show color variations. The controls for color transformations for the brush are located in the Color Dynamics section of the palette (see Figure 33). I set the Foreground/Background Jitter to 100%, so that there would be a shift between the foreground and background colors. Setting the two colors to opposing shades of green would add the randomness of color seen on a tree. True, all the leaves on a tree are a similar green; however, when viewing them at different angles, they reflect light and shadow creating the illusion of different colors.

The Hue Jitter was set to a low 12%. This added a slight variation to the colors being used. Large numbers introduce unwanted colors such as reds and blues.

The Saturation Jitter was set to 25% to produce more variety in the colors on the leaves. The Brightness Jitter was set to 10% for similar effects on the color variance.

32 The Shape Dynamics portion of the Brushes palette lets you set various different distortions for your brush.

33 The Color Dynamics section of the Brushes palette lets you set variations in the color that your brush is applying.

I chose a bright green for the Foreground color and a dark green for the Background color. The resulting stroke created a branch full of leaves like the one in Figure 34.

With all the parameters set, I saved it as a preset so that I could always call it up again. I saved it by choosing the Save Brush command in the Brushes window drop-down menu. This is also the place where you load other brushes you might have created.

Changing the Diameter in the Brush Tip portion of the palette changes the size of the brush. For instance, the same leaf brush set to 200% yields large leaves—as if you were up close to the tree. A small diameter of about 5% creates tiny leaves that appear far away.

Other forms of foliage are also a snap to reproduce with the custom brush presets. Grass is the perfect example. I used to create grass with polka-dotted brushes that faded out as I stroked across the canvas. This worked, but it created a translucency to the tips of the grass blades. It also required changing the fade-out rate often to get the grass texture to look varied. The new solution to this—you guessed it—Custom Brush Presets!

To reproduce grass, I created a custom brush shape by generating a clump of grass in a three-blade section using the Pen tool (Figure 35).

As in Figure 27, the paths were then filled with black on a separate transparent layer, selected, and then defined as a brush (Edit>Define Brush).

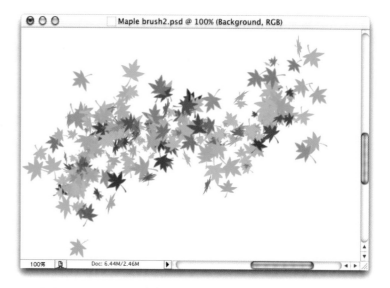

34 The brush now creates a lush tree branch in a single stroke.

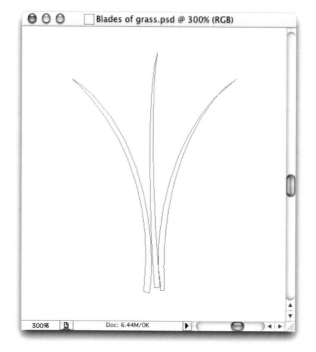

35 Three blades of grass are created with the Pen tool.

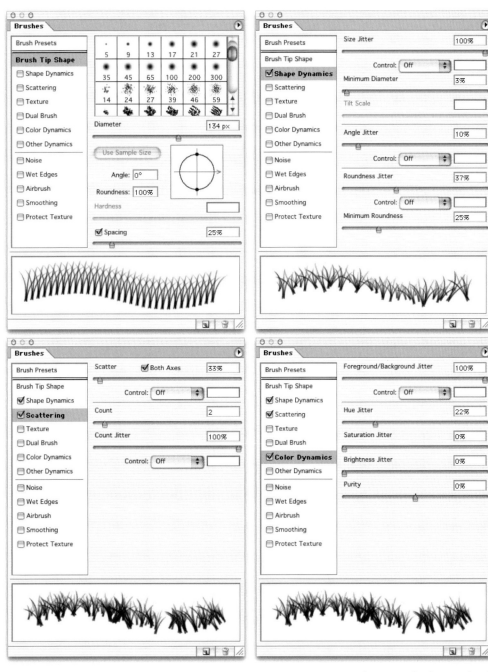

The brush was then given the attributes to make a realistic and believable lawn. The Shape Dynamics were set, as shown in Figure 36. Notice that the Angle Jitter is set at a low percentage. Unlike the previous brush, where the leaves are scattered in various directions, the blades of grass in this picture all need to point up. The low jitter setting produces a slight variation in angle, while remaining basically vertical.

36 The settings for the grass brush.

I chose a bright green for the Foreground color and a dark green for the Background color. By dragging the new brush across the screen back and forth, and from top to bottom, I was able to create a lawn that looked believable (Figure 37).

Grass can take on other shapes, such as the long dune grass that grows by the sea. For this type of grass, I created a single long blade of grass (Figure 38). Applying certain attributes gave me a brush that replicated the real thing (Figure 39).

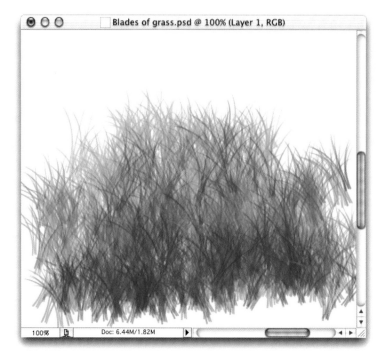

37 Dragging the grass brush across the canvas produces a realistic looking lawn.

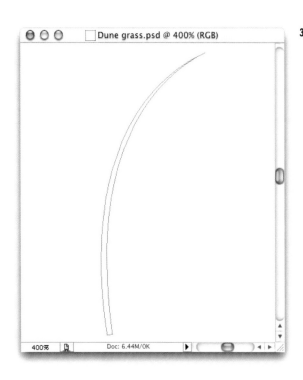

38 A single blade of grass is created to form the basis of the grass found growing on sand dunes.

39 Dragging the brush lays down a veil of soft dune grasses.

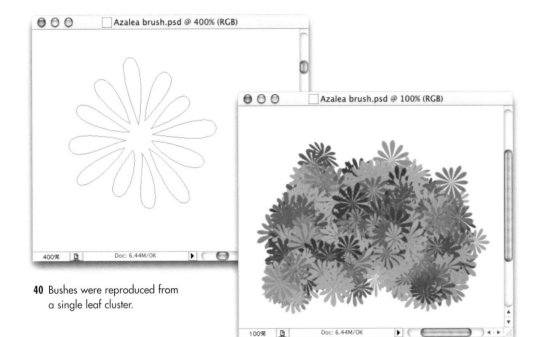

40 Bushes were reproduced from a single leaf cluster.

With this newfound technique for creating grass, I went foliage crazy! I walked around my garden just looking for plants that I could create brush presets for. I created a bush by creating a single leaf cluster and setting the parameters to simulate the growing patterns in nature.

NOTE   I am proud to say that Adobe has included my Maple leaf and Grass brushes as add-ons in the Photoshop 7 package. They can be found in the main Brushes palette. The Bush brush can be found in the Special Effects brushes. These are available through the Brushes window drop-down menu.

To create ivy, I needed to use another of the new functions available to custom brushes—Texture. I defined a pattern to replicate the characteristic bumpy texture of ivy leaves (Figure 41).

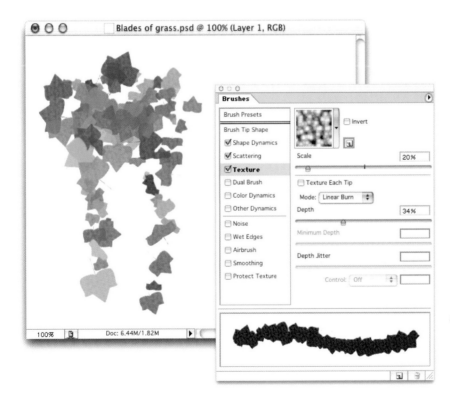

41 A texture was needed to replicate the bumpy surface found on an ivy leaf.

In the "late afternoon" image (on the cover), the stitching on the cloth draped over the dresser required a different brush preset (Figure 42).

I started out by creating a single stitch to serve as the brush shape (Figure 43).

In the Brushes palette, I gave it the attributes needed to make the elaborate needlework on the actual cloth. The parameters shown in Figure 44 randomized the stitches, ever so slightly, to give it realism. Most importantly, the Angle Jitter Control was set to Direction. This caused the angles of the brush tips to follow the direction of the stroke.

42 The stitching on the fabric over the dresser requires another brush preset.

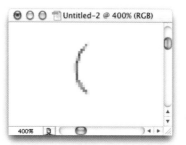

43 A single stroke is created for the basis of the stitch.

44 The settings for the stitch brush are subtle enough to simulate real-life stitching.

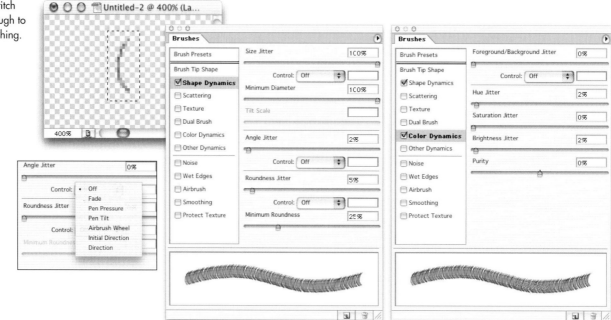

Using the Pen tool, I created paths in the working file that took on the shape of the stitch design (Figure 45). Those paths were then stroked with the custom stitch brush.

The highlights on the edges of the polished wood surfaces also required the use of a customized brush preset. The surface of the wood was not as smooth as you might expect. For one thing, the furniture is old. Time and the elements have affected the surface. Studying the scene, I noticed a roughness to the reflection of light on the edges (Figure 46). Using a standard brush would have created a smooth glow not consistent with the actual scene.

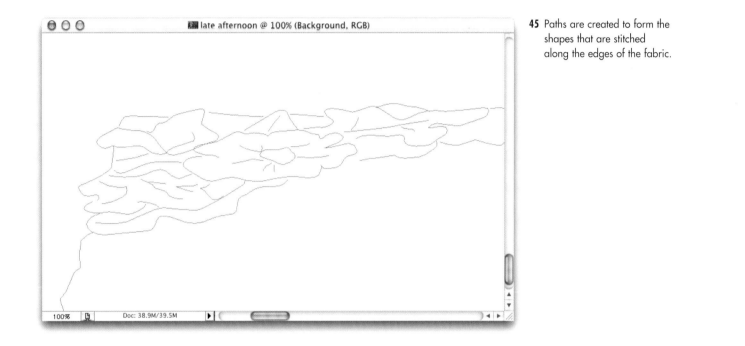

45 Paths are created to form the shapes that are stitched along the edges of the fabric.

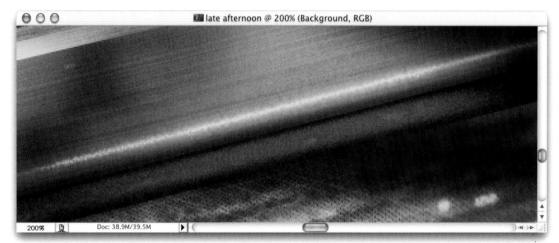

46 The reflections of light on the polished wood required a rough look that could easily be replicated with a custom brush preset.

I started with a brush that already existed—the Star 26 brush. The Star 26 brush was the basis for the kind of brush needed for the effect desired. The star brushes have rough outer edges that when smeared across the canvas, look rough along the edges of the stroke (Figure 47). A little modification in the Brushes palette was the only requirement.

The reflections fade out on both sides, so I created two paths to replicate the effect. The stroking of a path follows the direction in which the path was created. Creating two paths in opposite directions allowed me to reproduce the effect I was viewing in the real scene (Figure 48). Because the light seemed to fade out from the center, a fadeout was assigned to the brush. The paths were then stroked with the custom brush.

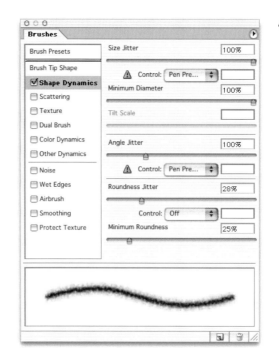

47 The shape of the brush is simple. It has the attributes assigned to it that give the desired effect.

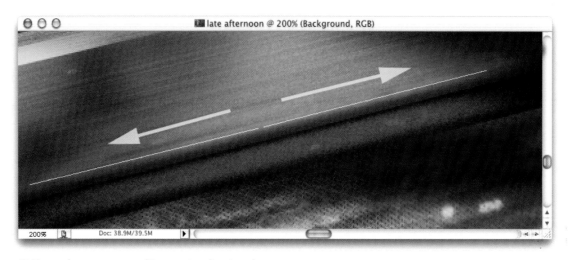

48 Two paths were generated in opposing directions that would then be stroked with the custom brush.

Up in Smoke

Smoke and clouds are two things that are very hard to illustrate. The randomness and texture needed for realism can be very difficult to achieve. Yep! However, once again brush presets come to the rescue!

49 The chimney needs smoke to billow from its top.

Using a combination of a soft-edged brush and some sneaky attributes, the process becomes effortless.

In Figure 49, I wanted some smoke to billow from the chimney. I experimented with various shapes and found the soft shape in Figure 50 to be the best starting point for creating smoke. I assigned the functions to the brush while keeping an eye on the preview at all times (Figure 51). I also wanted the smoke to grow in size like a real smoke, so I assigned a size to the stroke based on the stylus pressure.

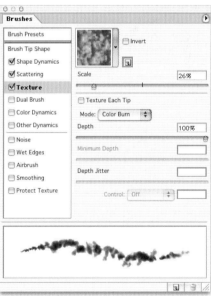

50 The shape of the brush has a soft edge.

51 The attributes assigned to the smoke brush.

For the first time, I utilized the Dual Brush feature (Figure 52). This feature allows you to pick a second brush to modify the original shape. The modifications can create many different effects based on the brush shape, frequency, and more importantly, the mode assigned to it.

NOTE Chapter 6, "Creating the Elements," shows you a different approach to the creation of smoke, because after all, smoke is never the same.

The moral of the story is that many elaborate effects that formerly required manipulation are now easily achieved with custom brushes. To make the process simple, you can preview the brush while it is clearly visible within the palette. So, play, play, and play some more.

52 The Dual Brush introduces a second brush shape that has an affect on the main shape being used.

53 The stroke is applied to complete the desired effect of smoke.

A Greener World: Creating Foliage

In the last chapter, you were introduced to Photoshop's fabulous new Paint Engine. You saw how easy it is to fill a tree full of leaves with a single stroke of the mouse. In this chapter, you take a closer look at the botanical wonders of the world. You use that custom brush for foliage, and you learn how to use it. You also create foliage that cannot be created with a custom brush. For example, it requires a little more effort to render the leaves so that they are closer to the viewer where details of a single leaf are seen.

I was born on 139th Street in Manhattan and I lived in New York City for 45 years. Trees were something I saw in books and on the occasional trip to Central Park. If you look at some of the paintings from my New York days in the gallery, you might notice that there is not much in the way of greenery in the scenes. I now live in a Redwood grove in the Berkeley Hills of California. I now see nothing but green around me.

This closeness to nature has had a strong effect on my art. It has also presented me with the challenge of creating foliage in a believable and realistic fashion. The randomness of shapes necessary to make foliage look real is one of the greatest challenges, and it requires the most effort to reproduce. However, the computer is supposed to make artists' lives easier. This chapter discusses my approaches and solutions to the problem of creating foliage.

Creating a Lifelike Tree

Being able to create a brush that fills a tree with leaves is just the beginning. The brush does not make a tree. That is your job.

The Paintbrush tool is used with various sizes of hard-edged brushes to render the basic shape of a tree, as shown in Figure 1.

Choosing a color to make the bark is next. In the case of the maple tree, I used a gray tone, as shown in Figure 2.

1 Using the Paintbrush tool, the basic shape of the tree is created.

2 A gray tone is used for the final color of the tree trunk.

To form the tree bark texture, I added noise with the Add Noise filter (Filter>Noise>Add Noise), as shown in Figure 3. Then, I applied the Texturizer filter (Filter>Texture>Texturizer) in Sandstone mode to complete the bark (Figure 4).

Using a soft-edged brush, details and shadows are added to the tree trunk and branches to give the tree dimension. The Dodge tool adds highlights along the front edge of the trunk (Figure 5).

3 The Add Noise filter is applied to the trunk to create a basic randomness to the gray tone.

4 The Texturizer filter completes the tree bark texture.

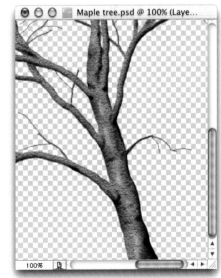

5 Using the Paintbrush and Dodge tool with varying sizes, dimension and additional detail are added to the tree.

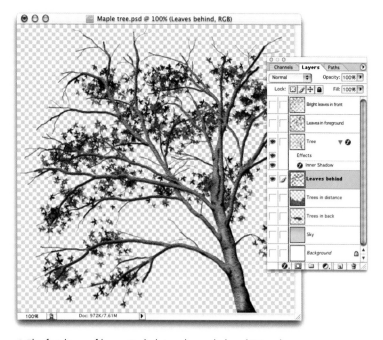

6 The first layer of leaves is dark in color and placed into a layer behind the tree layer.

The tree is now ready for some leaves. Using the maple leaf brush, which is discussed in Chapter 2, "The Art of Brush Making," leaves are added. Clusters of leaves are created in separate layers. The first cluster is created in a layer and placed behind the layer with the tree trunk, as seen in Figure 6. This layer is called Leaves behind. These leaves are given a darker tone to give the illusion of depth.

A second cluster is created in a new layer and placed in front of the tree layer. Using a set of bright red colors, leaves are added to the various branches of the tree, as seen in Figure 7. This is the Leaves in foreground layer. A third and final cluster of leaves is created in the topmost layer, as seen in Figure 8. This layer is called Leaves in front, and this is where the brightest leaves are added to finalize the tree.

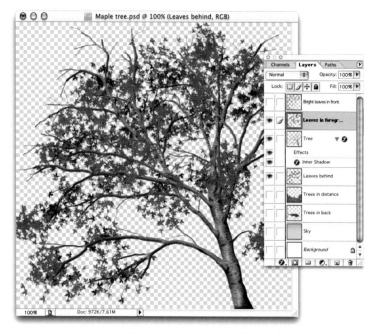

7 Bright red leaves are added to a layer in front of the tree layer.

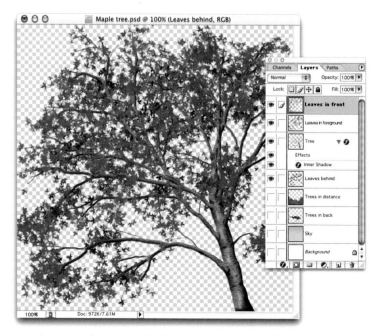

8 In the topmost layer, some final leaves are created using the brightest colors to denote highlighted leaves.

Additional trees and a sky are added to complete the scene, as shown in Figures 9–11. These background elements are placed in layers behind the layers that make up the tree.

9 Using a different leaf brush, small trees are added in a layer called Trees in distance, which is placed behind the layers that make up the tree.

10 In a layer named Trees in back, smaller and darker trees are added to represent trees that appear off in the distance.

11 The final layer is filled with a blue gradient to represent the sky.

Turning Over a New Leaf

The "Solano Grill" painting has a couple of small potted trees on both sides of the entrance and a partial view of a much larger tree framing the image on the left side (Figure 12). To create this foliage, a different approach is required. These are very specific types of trees. If I didn't create them as they really look, I am sure I would get emails from a score of horticulturists who might want to educate me about how the plant should look. Don't laugh, it happens.

I took a leaf from the actual site as a reference. It had fallen off the plant and was lying on the ground. (I didn't want you to think that I go around picking leaves off of other people's plants.) I also happen to have the smaller, potted trees in my own garden. The truth is, the potted tree in the painting is actually mine and not exactly the plant that was in front of the restaurant. Same type of plant, though. Using the Pen tool, I created paths for the shape of the leaf and the veins within it. I also created two leaves of different sizes and shapes to add variety to the basic shape. The outer path was filled with a green color. The paths for the veins were stroked with a darker shade of green. The path for the central vein system was filled with a yellow color. I added red color to the stem to match the leaves on the real tree. Figure 13 illustrates each of the windows.

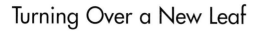

12 There are two different types of foliage visible in the "Solano Grill" image.

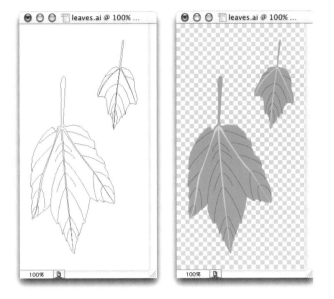

The two leaves are duplicated. The duplicated set is then distorted with the Scale tool (Edit>Transform>Scale), as shown in Figure 14.

The leaves are duplicated several times, and additional distortions, such as rotation (Edit>Transform>Rotate), distort (Edit>Transform>Distort), and scale (Edit>Transform>Scale) are applied. The modified leaves are arranged in various layers over the layer of the tree branches. This is the same layering technique that was applied to the maple tree at the beginning of this chapter.

Using the Dodge and Burn tools, shadows and highlights are added. This gives the leaves depth and additional variety, making them look like individual leaves rather than one leaf that has been copied. Wherever there was a leaf overlapping another leaf, I created a shadow on the leaf below. This gives the leaves a spatial relationship (Figure 15).

13 The window on the left shows the paths for the leaves. The window on the right shows the colors applied to the paths.

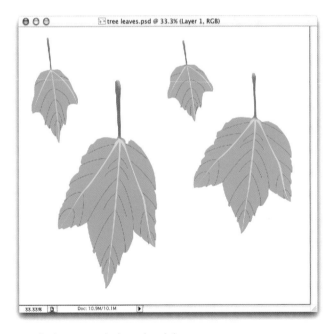

14 The leaves are duplicated and distorted to make them look different from the originals.

15 The leaves are placed as clusters into multiple layers, and then highlights and shadows are added.

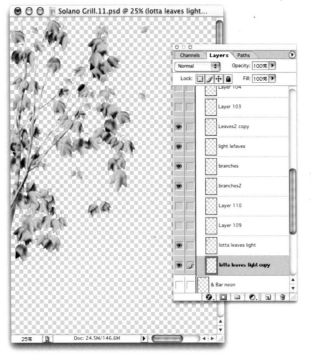

I adjusted the color and saturation in different layers to simulate depth. Using the Dodge and Burn tools, I then added shadows and highlights to selected leaves.

Figures 16 and 17 show various layers of the tree. Figure 18 shows all the layers that went into the creation of the final tree.

16 The light-colored leaves on the backside of the tree are visible, in addition to a few of the leaves in the front.

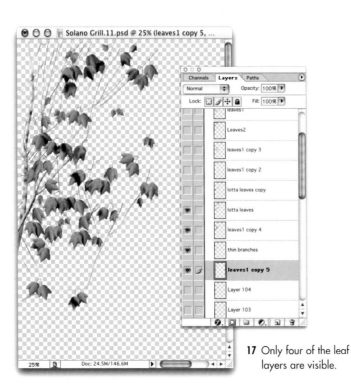

17 Only four of the leaf layers are visible.

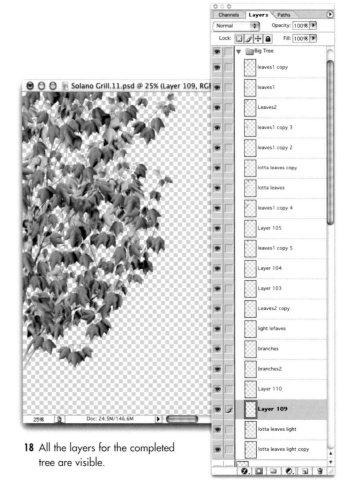

18 All the layers for the completed tree are visible.

Figure 19 is a close-up of the smaller plants on each side of the entrance. Though the shapes and color are different, the process for creating them is identical to the large tree.

Figures 20 through 23 show another example of the technique for creating foliage.

19 It takes several layers to complete the smaller plant.

20 A detail showing the bush in the Cedar image.

21 Paths for the basic leaf shape.

22 The paths are filled with color. The result is then duplicated and distorted.

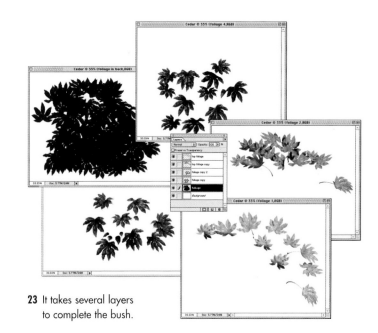

23 It takes several layers to complete the bush.

Redwoods

A Redwood tree has branches made up of several needles. Figure 24 shows the basic shape created to represent a single branch segment. In this particular painting, the shape was created in Illustrator. However, the process is the same as in the previous examples. The branches are constructed in several configurations (Figure 25) and imported into Photoshop where they are placed in position over the gate, as seen in Figure 26. Depth and shading are handled differently in this case.

Notice that there is very little color shift within the needles. Entire segments are colorized to conform to their relationship to the light source. Chapter 4, "Lights and Shadows," goes into more detail on this subject.

24 The shape for the Redwood branch is a series of filled paths.

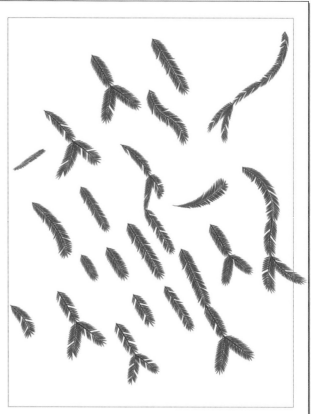

25 The shapes are distorted to add variety.

26 The shapes of the branches are imported into the Photoshop file and colorized again to conform to the lighting in the scene.

Lights and Shadows

I love the play of light on objects. Trying to re-create that interaction is always an enjoyable challenge. California gives me new insight into the effects of lights and shadows. The California sun is very bright and clear. It tends to overly saturate the colors of a scene. It also casts very sharp shadows.

Artificial light is also striking. It has competing light sources that illuminate a scene from different angles. This creates a myriad of shadows that clash and compete for prominence. Artificial light also comes in colors. Colored light sources create colored shadows.

Shadows add life and dimension to an image. Without them, an object appears flat. Shading a scene properly gives it the illusion that it has a third dimension. Lights and shadows determine the relationship of one object to another and their place in the total scene. The position and strength of the lights and shadows also set the overall mood of the image.

1 The noontime sun is directly above the tree, which causes the shadow to fall directly below the tree.

Photoshop is a two-dimensional program. Photoshop's files are configurations of pixels that are placed across the width and down the height of an image. There is no depth, as one would find in a 3D program. The illusion of a third dimension is created through the use of shading and perspective.

The image on the cover of this book is called "late afternoon." The angle and color of the light streaming in through the window identifies the time of day for the scene. The sun is low on the horizon. The late afternoon sun is turning to that orange color of a sun that is setting.

The position of shadows in an outdoor scene automatically establishes the time of day. Figure 1 shows a tree in a field at noon. How do we know it is noon? The shadow is directly below the tree, which means the sun is directly above the tree, as it would be at the noon hour. Figure 2 shows a scene that represents a time that is a little later in the day. The sun has moved from directly above the tree, and the shadow streams away from the tree. Figure 3 shows a scene that is set late in the day. The sun is low, causing the shadow to lengthen.

2 The afternoon sun is off to the left, causing the shadow to fall behind the tree and to the right of it.

3 The evening sun is low on the horizon, which results in a longer shadow. The setting sun also casts a warmer color over the scene.

Shadows are often the focus in some of my paintings. "Bodega shadows" and "shadowplay" are two very good examples of how shadows play a main role in some of my paintings (Figures 4 and 5).

4 The painting, "Bodega shadows," uses a shadow as the central focus.

5 In the "shadowplay" painting, the shadow is the subject.

The shadow starts as a shape that is outlined with the Pen tool. Figure 6 shows the paths created for the shadow shapes in Bodega shadows. In Figure 7, the path is turned into a selection and filled with a dark blue color.

The final touches are illustrated in Figure 8. Note that the opacity was lowered in this illustration. The layer was also blurred with the Gaussian Blur filter (Filter>Blur>Gaussian Blur).

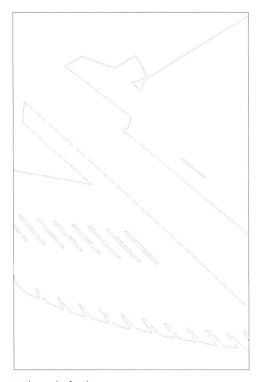

6 The paths for the shadow shapes.

7 The path is selected and filled with the color for the shadow.

8 The layer of the shadow is blurred and reduced in opacity.

Figure 9 shows the paths for the shadows in shadowplay. These shadows hint at the structure that isn't in view in the image. The paths are filled with black, and they are blurred. This is a similar procedure as the one used in the previous Bodega shadows example. The difference here is that the area where the shadows are cast is made up of uneven surfaces, opposed to a flat surface. The shadows are made larger than the area they will cover, and they are clipped with the layer that contains the surface shape. Figure 10 shows the shadows that are cast onto the wooden board along the top of the scene. Figure 11 shows the clipped shadow. Refer to Chapter 1, "Off to a Good Start," for more information on creating a clipping group.

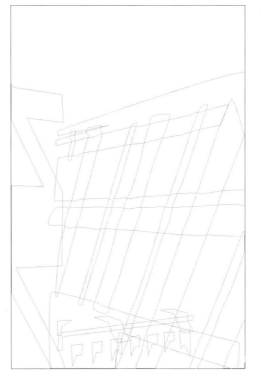

9 The paths for the shadows in the shadowplay example.

10 The shadow cast on the wooden board is put in a layer over the layer of the board.

11 The shadow is clipped by the layer of the wooden board.

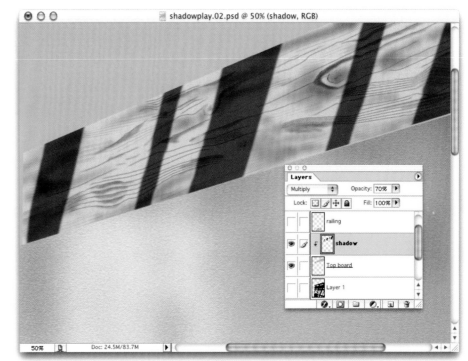

Figure 12 shows the larger shadow that is cast over the main part of the wall. Figure 13 shows the detail of the fence at the bottom of the image. Notice the shapes that the shadows take as they travel over and around the banister.

12 The large shadow over the main wall.

13 The shadow that is cast over the railing has to conform to the various angles that make up the construction of the railing.

14 The drop shadow is a commonly used design element.

15 The Drop Shadow blending option controls in the Layer Style dialog box.

Shadows with Layer Style

Up to this point, the shadows are created as separate shapes. Each is unrelated to the shapes in the scene and only hint at the shape of the objects casting them. There are times when the object casting the shadow is completely visible in the scene.

The traditional drop shadow is one of these instances in which the object casting the shadow is visible. The drop shadow is commonplace in today's design circles. Figure 14 shows a traditional drop shadow effect.

The drop shadow has the identical shape of the object casting it. The distance from one object to another object and the direction of the light source determine the position of the shadow. Layer Styles enable you to add a drop shadow to layers. The shadow is controlled in many ways. Figure 15 shows the Layer Style for the Drop Shadow blending option.

The position of the shadow is established by adjusting the Angle field's value in the Structure area of the dialog box. The distance determines how far the shadow falls from the object casting it. The Spread field works like the Hardness feature of the brushes—the higher the percentage, the harder the edge. The Size field allows you to control the size of the shadow.

The Quality section of the dialog box includes a Contour field that allows you to set parameters to control the shape of your shadow. In Figure 16, you see a drop shadow applied to a red circle. The Distance value is increased to add separation to clearly view what happens with the Contour control. In Figure 17, a contour is chosen (not the default contour) by clicking on the arrow bar located to the right of the Contour icon. Note the shape of the drop shadow. You are not bound by these presets. Clicking the Contour icon brings up the Contour Editor in which you can set your own parameters (Figure 18).

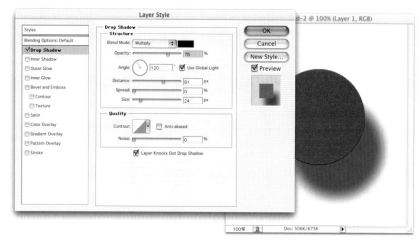

16 A drop shadow is applied to a layer in the Layer Style dialog box.

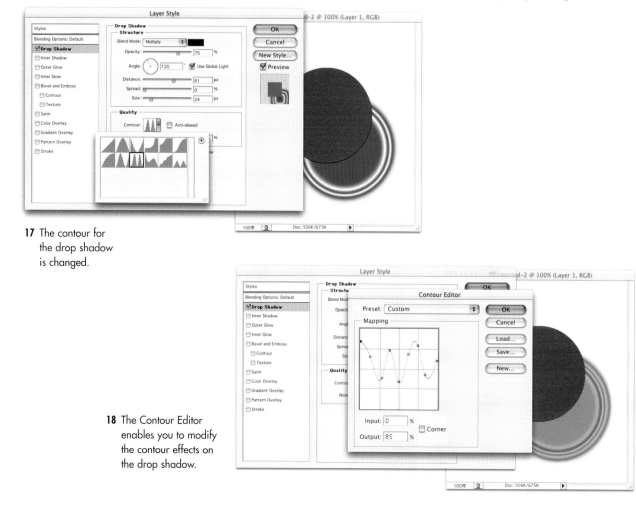

17 The contour for the drop shadow is changed.

18 The Contour Editor enables you to modify the contour effects on the drop shadow.

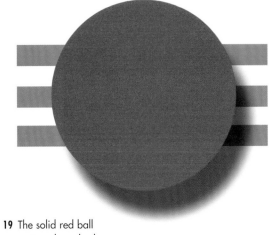

19 The solid red ball casts a drop shadow.

The Noise field enables you to set a noise level for the shadow, which aids in the prevention of banding. If you use the Add Noise filter, it applies the noise to the entire layer. In the Layer Style dialog box, the noise is applied to the shadow only.

The command at the bottom of the Drop Shadow dialog box, Layer Knocks Out Drop Shadow, sets the shadow's visibility when the object casting it is transparent. Figure 19 shows the red ball casting a shadow. In Figure 20, the Fill Opacity for the red ball is reduced to 40%. The drop shadow remains hidden behind the ball. In Figure 21, the Layer Knocks Out Drop Shadow button is deselected, which makes the shadow visible through the transparent ball.

20 The opacity for the red ball is lowered. The shadow remains dark, but is not visible through the ball.

21 With the Layer Knocks Out Drop Shadow option turned off in the Layer Style dialog box, you can now see the shadow through the transparent red ball.

In the Layer Style dialog box, there is a section for Blending Options. Here, you control General Blending and Advanced Blending options (Figure 22). In the General Blending section, you see the Opacity setting. You can set the opacity for the entire layer's content. In the Advanced Blending section, you see the Fill Opacity setting. This setting lets you lower the opacity of an object in the layer without changing the style effects (Figure 23).

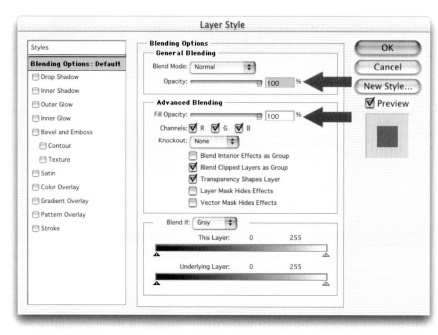

22 General Blending and Advanced Blending are two of the sections of the Layer Style dialog box.

23 The first ball on the left is the original object. The second is the one that has Layer Styles applied to it. The third is the ball that has an Opacity setting of 50%. The fourth ball has an Opacity setting of 100%, and the Fill Opacity setting is lowered to 50%.

24 The tree casts a shadow that travels across the ground and up the wall.

Distorted Shadows

Often, a shadow is distorted to such an extent that Layer Styles do not work. In such cases, the shadow has to be generated directly from the casting object and modified by hand. In Figure 24, the tree's shadow, if it is to look realistic, has to bend sharply where it meets the background wall.

To create this effect, the layer with the tree is duplicated. The Preserve Transparency option is turned on for the layer, and then it is filled with black. The black tree is then distorted (Edit>Transform>Distort). The distorted shape resembles the shadow traveling on the ground (Figure 25).

A second layer with another black-filled tree is placed in position where the shadow falls on the wall (Figure 26). It is reduced in size to simulate the effect of distance. Things appear smaller as they get farther away from the viewer. In Figure 27, you see the smaller black tree clipped by the layer of the wall.

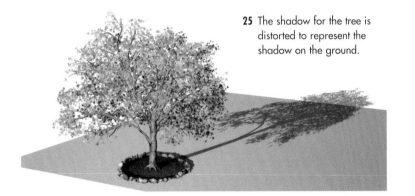

25 The shadow for the tree is distorted to represent the shadow on the ground.

26 A duplicate layer with the tree shadow is reduced in size to simulate distance, and it's placed so that its top half overlaps the base of the wall.

27 The layer of the wall clips the duplicate layer with the tree shadow.

The layer for the shadow created in Figure 25 is placed behind the layer with the wall. As a result, the wall hides the part of the shadow that is to be replaced by the shadow against the wall in Figure 27. It takes two shadows to create the illusion of a single shadow being cast on to two surfaces.

In Figure 28, a new ingredient is thrown into the mix—the wall is angled with respect to the tree and light source. This creates the effect of a lengthened shadow. The diagram in Figure 29 demonstrates the physics at work here.

28 Because the wall is positioned at an angle from the light source, the tree's shadow is elongated.

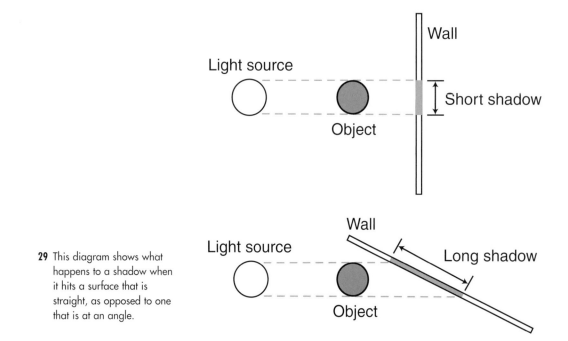

29 This diagram shows what happens to a shadow when it hits a surface that is straight, as opposed to one that is at an angle.

Creating Shadows

In the painting titled "Cedar," one of the more difficult effects that I tried to create was the shadow of a tree sweeping across the wall (Figure 30). The shadow is long because the light source is the setting sun, which is low on the horizon.

The tree itself is used to create the shadow. The tree trunk and the leaves are created in multiple layers that are merged together into a single layer once the tree is completed. This procedure is outlined in further detail in Chapter 3, "A Greener World: Creating Foliage," on creating foliage.

30 In the "Cedar" image, one of the more difficult effects that I tried to create was the shadow of the tree sweeping across the wall.

The layer that contains the merged tree is duplicated by dragging it over the Make New Layer icon at the bottom of the Layer's palette (Figure 31).

With Preserve Transparency turned on for the layer, fill it with black. Because the tree exists on a transparent layer, with Preserve Transparency turned on, when you select Edit>Fill, only the tree is filled. This black fill serves as the basis of the shadow (Figure 32).

NOTE   Preserve Transparency allows you to modify only the pixels in the layer that are active. The transparent area of the layer retains its transparency.

Preserve Transparency is turned off to apply a Blur filter to soften the shadow.

NOTE   The Blur filters create their effect inward and outward from the edge of the object being blurred. A Gaussian Blur of 10 softens the edge by 5 pixels inward and by 5 pixels outward. If Preserve Transparency is turned on, the outward effect is disabled. This looks very unnatural.

Use the Scale tool (Edit>Transform>Scale) to stretch the black tree to the width of the entire image (Figure 33). This achieves an effect of a long shadow across the wall.

The shadow is supposed to darken the underlying layers. To achieve this effect, the mode for the layer is changed to Multiply. This mode actually multiplies the brightness values of the pixels with the pixels under it. This considerably darkens the layers underneath the shadow. Finally, the Opacity was lowered so that the shadow would soften.

31 The layer that contains the merged tree is duplicated.

32 With Preserve Transparency turned on for the layer, it is filled with black.

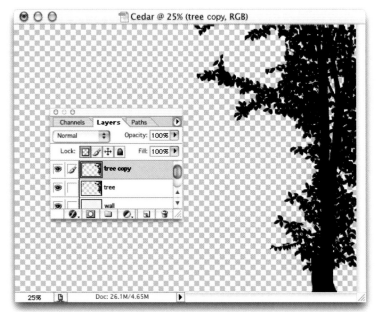

33 Using the Scale tool, the black tree is stretched to the width of the entire canvas.

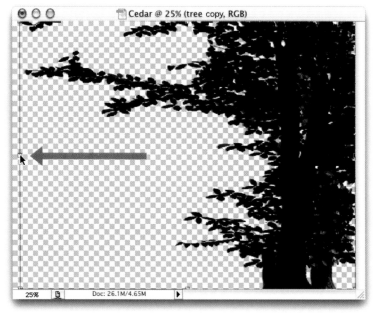

34 An alpha channel is created with a horizontal gradient from white to black.

35 The effect of the Motion Blur filter softens and stretches the shadow as it gets further away from the tree.

36 A gradient is created in the layer mask that went from gray to white.

© Bert Monroy 1998

37 The painting "handles" has shadows that travel down the face of the cabinet and then bend onto the floor.

Because the shadow is long and casts against a wall at an angle, the shadow must blur out more at the outer edges than the area immediately behind the tree. It also appears to stretch as it gets further away from the source. To help achieve this effect, an alpha channel is created with a horizontal gradient from white to black (Figure 34).

The alpha channel is then loaded as a selection. In this way, the left side of the image is fully selected, but the selection becomes weaker as it moves closer to the right side. A Motion Blur filter is applied to the layer of the shadow, as shown in Figure 35. Thanks to the selection, the more distance from the tree, the stronger the effect. The result is the desired effect—a stretched and blurred shadow that is cast by the tree across the wall. Deselect the gradient before proceeding.

As a shadow moves away from its source, it gets lighter. To achieve this effect here, a layer mask with a gradient is applied.

In a layer mask, black hides the contents of the layer; white makes them visible. I did not want the shadow to completely disappear, so I created a gray to white gradient in the layer mask rather than a black to white gradient, as shown in Figure 36. This gradually lightens the shadow as it moves to the left.

The painting "handles" also has long shadows that bend to the contours of the objects they are cast onto (Figure 37). The same procedure that used two shadows to simulate one is used here.

Double Your Pleasure

The "marble and matches" image introduces a new interaction of light and shadow—two light sources (Figure 38). This is evident by the shadow of the match that is leaning against the matchbox.

The first light source shines from above, just slightly to the rear of the objects. It is the stronger of the two light sources. The second light is coming from the front and to the left of the set of objects. This one casts a softer, lighter shadow. The two shadows actually intersect at the lower-front edge of the matchbox. The area where they intersect is darker.

38 The "marble and matches" image introduces a new interaction of light and shadow—two light sources.

The shadow of the matchstick that is leaning against the matchbox goes through an additional transformation. Because it leans away from the surface, the shadow is softer as it moves further away from the matchstick (Figure 39). This is the same behavior that you saw in the shadow of the tree in the beginning of this chapter.

The area where the shadow falls was selected (Figure 40). I saved the selection to an alpha channel, as shown in Figure 41. In this new channel, I filled the selected area with a gradient that is white to give it a stronger effect at the points that are further away from the match (Figure 42). Then, I deselected the area, returned to the color document, and loaded the alpha channel as a selection. I then applied a blur that, thanks to the selection, diverted focus from the shadow as it moved away from the match.

39 The shadow of the matchstick that is leaning against the matchbox requires additional work. Because of the lean in it's position, the shadow gets softer as it moves further away from the matchstick.

40 The area where the shadow falls is selected.

41 The selection is then saved to an alpha channel.

42 In the alpha channel, a gradient is laid down to give the strongest effect at the point in the shadow that is furthest away from the light source.

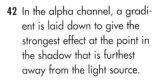

A Shadow from Glass

The marble in the "marble and matches" image requires additional effects for its shadow. The marble is made of transparent blue glass that allows light to pass through it. The density of the material, however, holds back some transference of the light. The color of the marble also affects the color of its shadow.

The main shadow is first. Using the Elliptical Marquee tool, on a new layer, I drew an oval with a slight feather to soften the edges (Figure 43). It was filled with a dark blue color.

The other objects in this painting are opaque. They block light, and therefore, they cast neutral shadows. In creating them, I used a black fill. The marble, however, is partially transparent. It allows some blue light to pass through it, which alters the color of the shadow. That is why the dark blue fill is needed.

The blue haze caused by the refracted light is created next. I created a narrower oval in the area of the marble's shadow and saved it into an alpha channel (Figure 44). Next, I created another narrower oval, which I saved into a second alpha channel (Figure 45). Then, the oval is heavily blurred (Figure 46). Using the Calculations command, the blurred channel is then subtracted from the original alpha channel, as shown in Figure 47. This gives a mask, which is saved into a third alpha channel to increase the softness of the effect at the center of the oval (Figure 48). This mask channel is then blurred again to soften the overall effect, as shown in Figure 49.

43 In a new layer, an oval is selected with a slight feather to the edges.

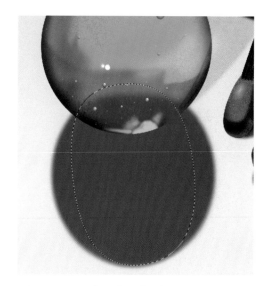

44 A narrow oval is selected in the area of the marble's shadow.

45 The selected oval is saved as a selection into an alpha channel, and then it is blurred.

46 Another narrower oval is created, saved to an alpha channel, and then heavily blurred.

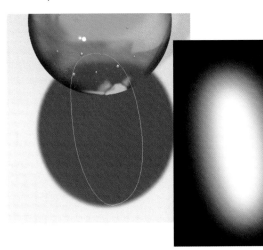

Calculations

Source 1: Untitled-1
Layer: *Merged*
Channel: Alpha 2   ☐ Invert

Source 2: Untitled-1
Layer: Layer 4
Channel: Alpha 3   ☐ Invert

Blending: Subtract
Opacity: 100 %
☐ Mask...

Result: New Channel

OK
Cancel
☑ Preview

47 Using the Calculations command, the narrowest, heavily blurred channel is subtracted from the original, narrow alpha channel. The results are sent to a new channel.

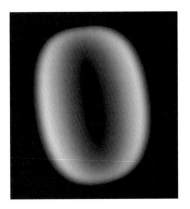

48 The Calculations command result gives a mask that increases the softness of the effect at the center of the oval.

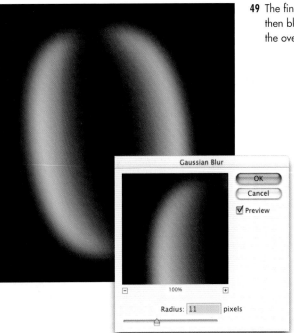

Gaussian Blur

OK
Cancel
☑ Preview

100%

Radius: 11 pixels

49 The final channel is then blurred to soften the overall effect.

In the RGB channels, a new layer is created. The mask channel is loaded as a selection and filled with a blue color that is lighter than the previously used one (Figure 50). This superimposes a light blue highlight on the shadow underneath it.

As a final touch, the highlights visible within the shadow are created with a soft-edged paintbrush, which uses various shades of light blue and white.

Another example of light that travels through transparent objects is reflected in the image named ointment (Figure 52). In this image, the shadow of the glass applicator runs across the cork (Figure 53). The applicator is made of clear glass, so colorization of the shadow is not necessary.

In this case, the applicator acts as a magnifying glass that concentrates the light in a bright streak.

To create this effect, I employed the Paintbrush tool. I set the brush to fade out (run out of paint) at a specified time (Figure 54). In a new layer, a fade-out stroke is created using a yellow color. The fade distance is decreased and white is used to create a second streak. This completes the effect.

With the Shift key down, I clicked with the Paintbrush tool at the base where the highlight began and then again at the other end of the top of the cork following the direction of the shadow. The result was light shining through the glass applicator.

NOTE If you press the Shift key while using a tool, you achieve a straight line from click to click.

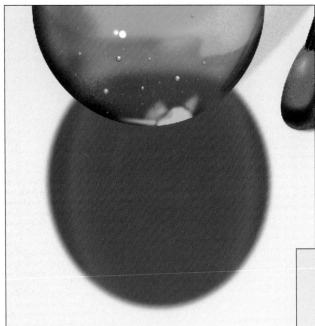

50 The channel is converted into a selection and filled with a blue color that is lighter than the one previously used to create the shadow.

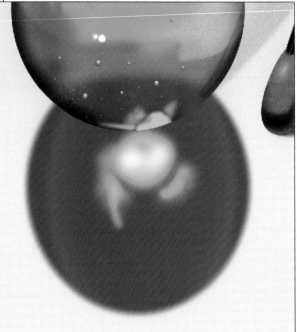

51 The highlights visible within the shadow are created with the Airbrush tool, which uses various shades of light blue and white.

52 This picture shows another example of light that travels through transparent objects. Here, the shadow of the glass applicator runs across the cork.

53 This close-up shows the shadow that is cast over the cork.

54 In the Brushes palette, I set the brush to Fade (run out of paint).

Shadows on Angled Surfaces

Shadows that fall on angled surfaces distort to follow the angles. Earlier in this chapter, the distortion of a tree casts a shadow across the ground and up a wall. The "Rendez-vous" image has a shadow that applies this technique to many surfaces simultaneously (Figure 55).

If you zoom in to the sign on the sidewalk, you see the play of shadows resulting from the chain (Figure 56).

As with the layer of the tree in the previous example, the layer of the chain is duplicated and filled with black to serve as the Shadow layer. This Shadow layer is duplicated several times because the shadow falls on different elements in the image. Each new element has its own angle.

The first angle requires the Shadow layer to be skewed downward, as shown in Figure 57.

It is then scaled down (Edit>Transform>Scale) horizontally to make it thinner. The fact that the wooden post, on which the shadow is cast, is at an angle to the light source causes the shadow to shrink. To see the shadow in the area of the wooden post only, the layer of the shadow and the sign are made into a clipping group.

55 The "Rendez-vous" image has a series of shadows that add drama and give a sense of the time of day.

56 The shadow that is cast by the chain is broken as it passes over various surfaces.

On the lower support bar of the sign, two shadows are added. The first follows the angle of the chain as it is cast on for the upper edge of the board. The angle is similar to the angle of the ground. The second goes through the same transformation as the one on the upper post (Figure 58).

The final shadow on the sidewalk is simply scaled down to make it smaller. A slight Blur filter is applied to soften it, as shown in Figure 59.

57 The Shadow layer is skewed downward.

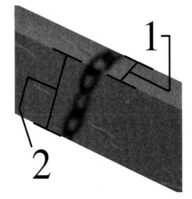

58 On the lower support bar of the sign, two shadows are added. The first is straight on for the upper edge of the board. The second one goes through the same transformation as the one on the upper post.

59 The shadow on the sidewalk is scaled down to make it smaller, and a Blur filter is applied to soften it.

Let There be Light

Until now, you have learned about shadows, but the title of this chapter is "Lights and Shadows." What about the lights? There are times when the light source is in the image. Other times, it is outside of the viewing area, but makes a cameo appearance somewhere in the image. The painting on the cover is a good example of the latter.

The image on the cover of the book depicts a scene that is lit by the late afternoon sun. The sun is the light source. It is located outside of the window, way off on the horizon. If you look closely at the edges of the mirror, you see the sun reflected on one of the angles (Figures 4.60 and 4.61).

60 The sun is visible on the edges of the mirror.

61 Darkening the other layers makes the sun easier to see.

Creating that tiny reflection of light (the sun) is an easy task. Two clicks with the Paintbrush tool is all it takes. The first click is the large brush with a soft edge. This creates the glare effect. The second click is the smaller, hard-edged brush that represents the sun.

I use this technique in many of my paintings. Figure 62 shows the "Studio theater" painting, which utilizes this technique several times.

Have you ever attempted to take a picture of the sun? It's a bit hard on the film. Likewise, I tend to stay away from including the sun in the painting. The moon, on the other hand, is a great light source because it can be placed directly in view without blinding the viewer. The moon also has different reactions to the atmosphere, creating some cool effects.

62 The sun's light is visible in several places in this painting.

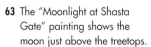

63 The "Moonlight at Shasta Gate" painting shows the moon just above the treetops.

In the "Moonlight at Shasta Gate" painting, the moon is visible above the treetops (Figure 63). It is a clear night, and the shadows that are cast over the road are crisp. Note the tiny reflections of the moon on the shiny leaves of the bushes next to the road (Figure 64).

64 The bushes next to the road have shiny leaves that reflect the moon.

65 The "night walk" painting has a halo around the moon.

In the "night walk" painting, there is a halo around the moon, as shown in Figure 65. High in the atmosphere, under certain conditions, ice crystals form—millions of them. As the light of the moon passes through these crystals, it is refracted, hence the halo. I was stunned the first time I saw this!

The moon is placed in a layer above the layer that contains a deep blue gradient for the sky (Figure 66).

A bright blue color is selected for the Foreground color. Using the Gradient tool (Figure 67), in Radial Gradient mode (Figure 68), set the gradient for Foreground to Transparent (Figure 69).

66 The moon is placed in a layer above the layer with the blue gradient for the sky.

67 The Gradient tool is selected.

68 Radial Gradient is chosen for the technique.

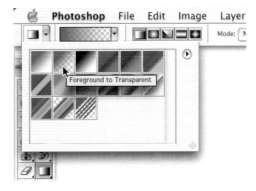

69 Foreground to Transparent is chosen for the type of gradient.

A small, circular gradient is created in a new layer that is behind the layer of the moon (Figure 70).

The opacity for the layer with the gradient is decreased to soften the effect (Figure 71).

Using the Elliptical Marquee tool, a large circle is selected around the moon. This circle is the basis for the halo that surrounds the moon in the painting, as shown in Figure 72.

The halo is a ring around the moon. The current selection is a big circle so it is necessary to modify the selection. Select Border from the Select menu (Select>Modify>Border), as shown in Figure 73. I set this at a high number, 40 pixels.

70 A gradient is created behind the moon.

71 The opacity is decreased for the layer with the gradient.

72 A large circle is selected around the moon to serve as the basis for the halo.

73 Choose Border from the Select menu to outline the selected area.

74 The selection is filled with a soft blue color.

75 The opacity is decreased to soften the halo.

NOTE Values entered in dialog boxes that are specified in pixels are dependent on the resolution of the image you are working on. For example, if you want an effect to occur over a half-inch area, then you should set your pixel dimension based on the resolution. 72 dpi requires a measurement of 36 pixels to achieve a half-inch; 300 dpi requires 150 pixels.

Apply a feathered edge to the selection to soften it (choose Select>Feather). I gave it a feather of 20, which is half the amount of the border size.

In a new layer, the selection is filled with a soft blue color, as shown in Figure 74.

The opacity is decreased for the layer of the halo to soften the glow, as shown in Figure 75.

Figure 76 shows the painting "view1." In this picture, the moon is visible through the fog. The process is identical to the one shown in Figures 67–70. The moon itself has no detail and is simply a white circle. There is a small, dark glow around the moon, which is then surrounded by the larger, light-colored glow.

76 The "view1" painting shows the moon through the fog.

A Bright Spot

Artificial light is not as blinding as looking directly into the sun. This does not mean that I recommend you stare at a light bulb. The painting, "the gate," uses the light source as the main focal point. In fact, without the light source, this particular scene is quite dark at night.

The light that is emitted from the lantern creates interesting effects as it cascades over the various surfaces surrounding it. Being true to these effects makes the scene realistic.

77 The painting, "the gate," uses the light source as the main focal point.

First, look at the effect on the foliage. How the foliage is created is discussed in Chapter 3, "A Greener World: Creating Foliage." Notice that the Redwood branches hanging over the light are both a light and dark green (Figure 78). The light green branches are the ones behind the light. The dark green branches are between you, the viewer, and the light source.

The dark needles on the branches in the front have a slightly lighter-colored edge to them. This results from the roundness at the edges of the needles. Because of this, the needles pick up a glow from the light around the edges.

Anti-aliasing is applied to the needles. This ensures that they appear smooth and unpixelated. In this case, the anti-aliasing makes it easy to achieve the effect of the edge's glow. The layer of the dark leaves is duplicated. The layer in back is filled with a bright green. The bright green color bleeds through the anti-aliasing of the dark needles in the front layer.

Figure 79 shows the branch as it was originally created. Figure 80 shows the duplicated branch with the brighter colors. Figure 81 shows the darkened branch in the top layer. Figure 82 shows both layers with the bright layer in back bleeding through on the edges of the dark layer in front. If the effect of the lightened edges is not strong enough for your purposes, it can be enhanced. Make the topmost layer, or the darkest leaves, a selection. Use the Contract feature (Select>Modify>Contract) to shrink the selected area. Inverse the selection (Select>Inverse), and then press Delete to make the outside edges of the dark leaves smaller, allowing the brighter leaves to show through the darker ones.

78 The Redwood branches hanging over the lantern reflect the light based on their position to it.

79 The original branch in a layer.

80 The duplicated layer in back has brighter colors.

81 The top layer is darkened.

82 The two layers are visible.

The top of the gate is handled in a slightly different way. In Figure 83, you see how the top edges of the wooden boards pick up the light. You also see the bounce-back of the light from the cross-beam on the boards.

Creating the bright edges at the top of the boards requires a special mask. A layer style does not work in this case because the effect is not evenly distributed over the surface of the wooden boards.

Then, the boards are turned into a selection by Command-clicking (Control on PC) on them in the Layers palette. The selection is saved to an alpha channel (Select>Save Selection), as seen in Figure 84.

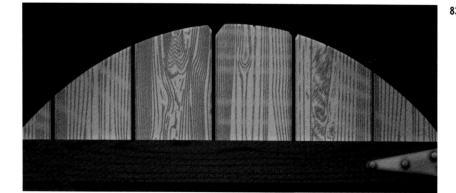

83 The close-up of the top of the gate reveals light being reflected on the wooden boards.

84 An alpha channel is created for the wooden boards.

85 The alpha channel is duplicated and blurred.

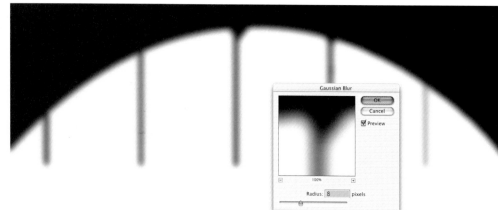

The alpha channel is duplicated. The duplicate is given a Gaussian Blur (Filter>Blur>Gaussian Blur), as seen in Figure 85. With the Move tool, the blurred copy is positioned to create an overlap between it and the original sharp-edged alpha channel. The reason you blur the channel is to create a softer effect for the bottom edge.

With the Calculations command, subtract the sharp channel from the blurred channel, as seen in Figure 86. Figure 87 shows you the result—a mask that exposes the edges of the top of the boards, and that is saved as a third alpha channel. You can now apply this mask (Select>Load Selection), and lighten it or color it as much as you want.

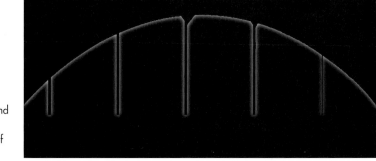

86 The Calculations command is used to subtract one alpha channel from another one to produce a mask.

87 The result of the Calculations command renders a mask that exposes the top lip of the boards.

The bounce-back of the light that is reflected on the boards from the crossbeam is a bit simpler. I chose an orange color similar to the one at the top of the boards in the last technique. Using a soft-edged brush, I painted a line straight across the edge of the board (Figure 88).

The mode for the layer is changed to Overlay (Figure 89). Its Opacity setting is decreased. The layer is then moved between the layer of the boards and the layer of the crossbeam. The final result is what you saw in Figure 83.

88 With a soft-edged brush, a line is drawn across the board.

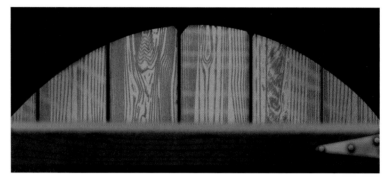

89 The mode for the layer is changed to Overlay, which gives the stripe a glow.

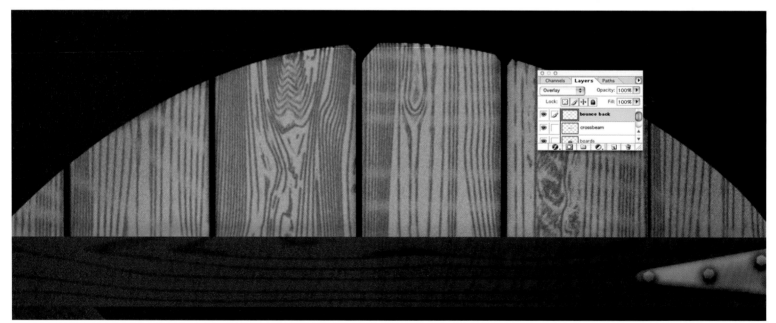

What's It Made Of? Creating Textures

Creating textures is a lot of fun. Sure, in a painting, textures create the illusion that objects are made of different materials. For example, we recognize the difference between a wooden fence and a stone wall. However, textures also have uses that go far beyond the realm of the usual Photoshop image. There is a whole market out there that involves plain textures.

We all experience the magic that computer graphics bring to the world of motion pictures. And what about games? We certainly see the revolution in the gaming world as well. Remember the old Pong game? A little blip moved back and forth across the screen while the user whacked it with a flat, vertical line that served as the paddle. Today, you can travel through mystical worlds in games that stagger the imagination. Sure, these movies and games are created in very sophisticated 3D environments; however, the textures on those walls and floors start off as simple Photoshop textures. This chapter walks you through some of the basic concepts behind the creation of textures.

Creating Realistic Wood Textures

In my last book, I dedicated an entire chapter to the creation of wood grain textures. Photoshop 6.0 introduced the Liquify command that made most of my previous wood grain techniques obsolete. In Photoshop 7.0, the Liquify command is located in the Filter menu instead of the Image menu (Figure 1). In addition to its new home, the Liquify command also has new functionalities. Figure 2 outlines the various tools in the Liquify dialog box.

The term liquify conjures up the sense of fluid motion or the distortion of an image. That is in fact what the Liquify command does.

With this in mind, you will find many uses for the Liquify tool. Creating wood grain is just the tip of the iceberg. In the next chapter, I show you how to use this feature to create other elements, such as fire and smoke.

1 The Liquify command appears as a subset of the Filter menu.

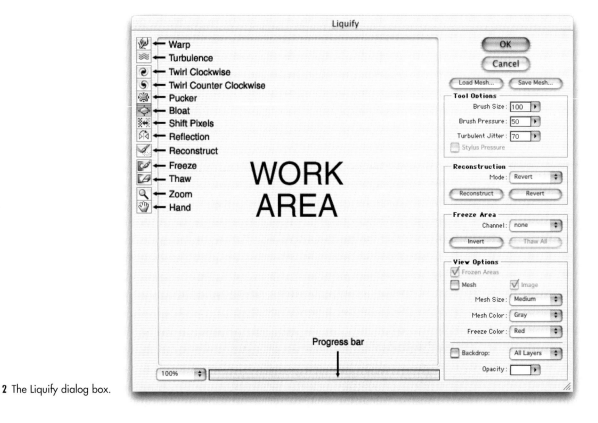

2 The Liquify dialog box.

The "Solano Grill" painting (Figure 3) includes a wooden door, as well as a trellis, visible on the far right side of the image. The close-up views of these show their detail (Figures 4 and 5). The process for creating these starts very much the way I would create simple wood grain in the past. I applied the Add Noise and Motion Blur filters to a selected area.

3 The "Solano Grill" painting uses the Liquify command to render the various wood surfaces of the door's frame and the trellis.

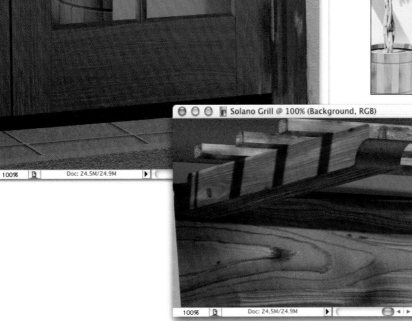

4 and 5 Details of the Solano Grill's wooden textures.

6 The Path tool is used to create the shape of the door's frames.

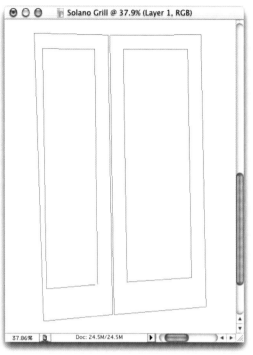

First, the shape of the doors was created with the Path tool (Figure 6). In a separate layer, these paths were filled with the basic wood color (Figure 7).

In another new layer, I created a large panel with the Rectangular Marquee selection tool (Figure 8). I then filled in this area with the same color of wood as the one used for the door's shape. The area was larger than the actual section of the door where it appeared. I wanted to create a single, textured area that was large enough to duplicate to all of the door's components. The Motion Blur filter also has peculiarities that make it difficult to work with a same-size selection.

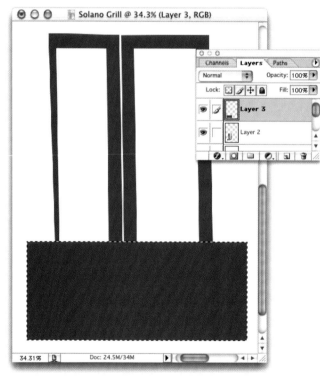

7 The paths are filled with a brown color to form the basis of the door's texture.

8 In a separate layer in the document, a shape is filled with the same color of brown as the doors. This layer is where the actual texture is created.

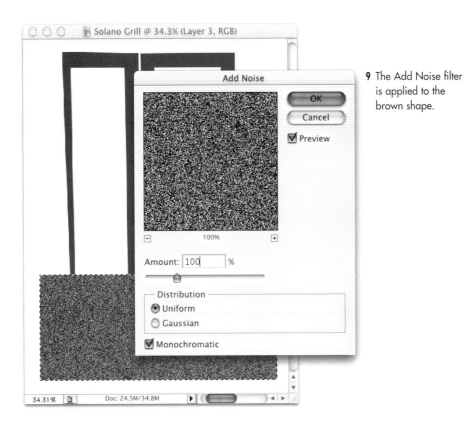

9 The Add Noise filter is applied to the brown shape.

The Add Noise filter (Filter>Add Noise) was then applied (Figure 9). A high percentage value was entered for the amount to produce a strong texture. The Monochromatic option was selected to eliminate the introduction of colors that weren't one of the browns of the wood. Uniform was selected for the Distribution. This softened the contrast between the varying shades of brown and reduced the amount of white introduced by the filter.

The Motion Blur filter (Filter>Blur>Motion Blur) was applied next (Figure 10). The Angle was set to 0 to constrain the streaks to a horizontal plane. The Distance was set to a higher number. This lengthened the streaks to better simulate a wood grain.

NOTE The Motion Blur filter bleeds color from outside of the selected area into the selected shape. This is why a larger area than necessary was selected to hold the texture. Notice the strange-looking effect on both sides of the selection in Figure 10.

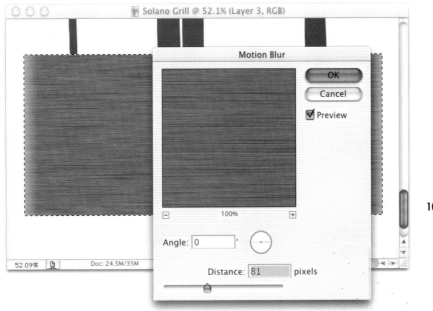

10 The Motion Blur filter is applied to streak the noise and simulate the wood grain.

11 Using the Levels command, I increased the contrast of the streaked Noise layer to enhance the texture. This also added an attractive color variation.

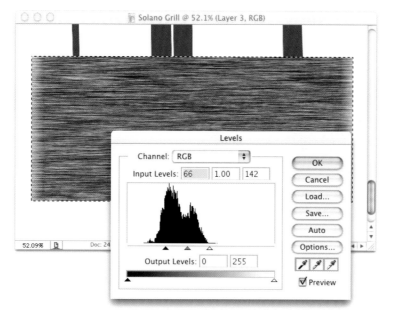

Using the Levels command (Image>Adjustments>Levels), I increased the contrast to emphasize the streaks of the grain (Figure 11). The texture is now good enough for most instances where wood grain is desired. Figures 12 and 13 show examples of this. The case is different for the "Solano Grill" image. In this picture, large sections of wood consist of a knotty wood grain texture.

Now comes the Grand Finale for the wood grain—the Liquify command (Filter>Liquify). The layer with the motion-blurred noise is activated and the Liquify command is selected. Using the Liquify Warp tool and a large-sized brush, I pushed the grain back and forth to create the grain's distortion (Figure 14). With the Turbulence tool, I added additional shivers and irregularities to the lines (Figure 15). Finally, with the Bloat tool, I added knots to some of the areas along the surface of the wood (Figure 16).

12 Two other areas in the "Solano Grill" image contain wood grains that are created using only the Add Noise/Motion Blur combination.

13 Another example of the use of this technique is the matchsticks in the "marble and matches" image. They are also created with the Add Noise/Motion Blur combination.

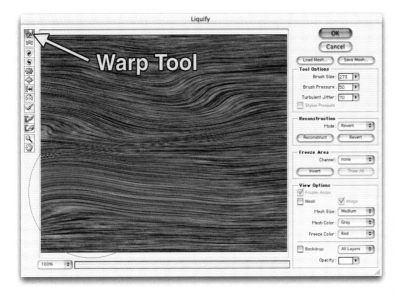

14 In the Liquify dialog box, the Warp brush is used to smear some of the wood grain to add a wavy appearance.

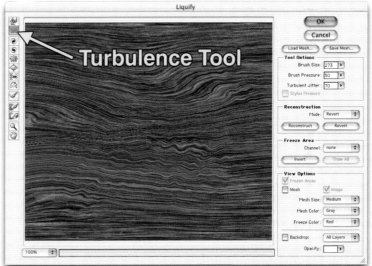

15 The Turbulence brush adds more waviness to the grain.

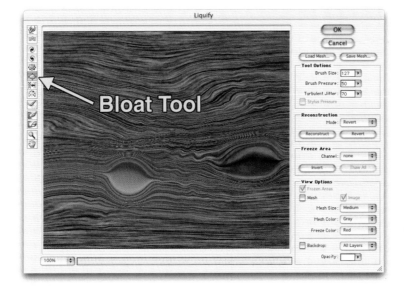

16 The Bloat brush spreads areas out to simulate where knots would appear on the wood surface.

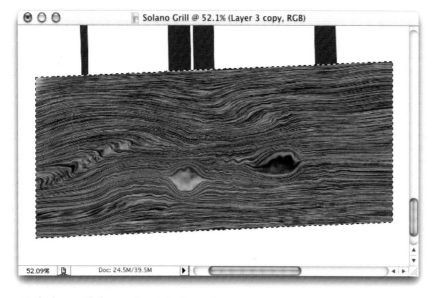

17 The layer with the wood grain is distorted to conform to the angles of the doorframe.

The layer with the wood is then duplicated and placed into position over the doorframe. Clipping it with the layer of the doorframe makes it visible through the shape of the door. Using the Distort function (Edit>Transform> Distort) I distorted the layer containing the wooden texture to follow the angles of the doorframe (Figure 17). The same was done with the duplicated wood grain layer over the other parts of the door.

NOTE Clipping a layer with another layer is covered in the "Clipping Group" section of Chapter 1, "Off to a Good Start."

The duplicated layer with the grain is rotated. The rotated grain is used in the vertical portions of the doors (Figure 18).

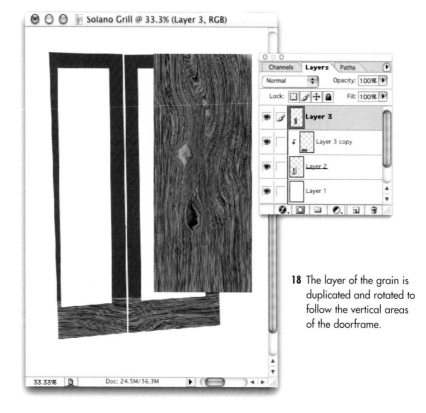

18 The layer of the grain is duplicated and rotated to follow the vertical areas of the doorframe.

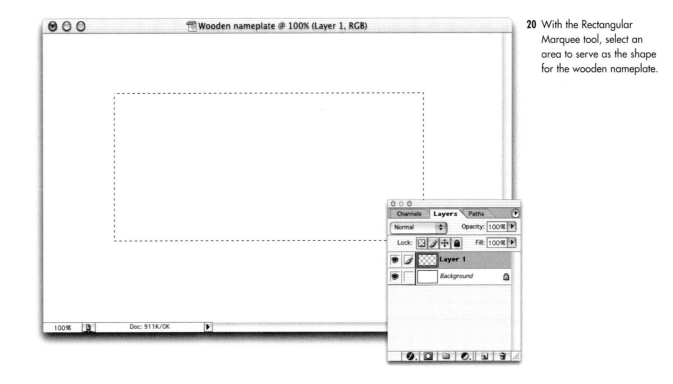

19 Start a new Photoshop file and set the parameters shown here.

Let's try this step-by-step exercise that will familiarize you with the technique.

We are going to create a wooden nameplate. The first thing we'll do is create the wood texture.

Create a new file in Photoshop with the dimensions shown in Figure 19.

Make a new layer by clicking the Make New Layer icon at the bottom of the Layers palette. This layer serves as the shape of the nameplate.

Choose a brown color that is appropriate for wood.

Using the Rectangular Marquee selection tool, select a shape that is centered in your document window. Leave at least an inch on each of the sides (Figure 20).

Fill the selection with the brown color.

20 With the Rectangular Marquee tool, select an area to serve as the shape for the wooden nameplate.

Create another new layer. Create a similar selection, but make it larger than the first rectangle and with the sides extending well beyond the dimensions of the original plate. Fill this selected area with the same brown color (Figure 21).

The larger size is necessary, as was the case with the shape in Figure 10. This is because the second filter you will use takes color from the outside edges of the selection and pulls that color into the selected area. You will discard these edge areas.

Choose the Add Noise filter (Filter>Noise>Add Noise). Make the value for the filter a large number (at least 100%), and click OK. This produces a rough texture (Figure 22).

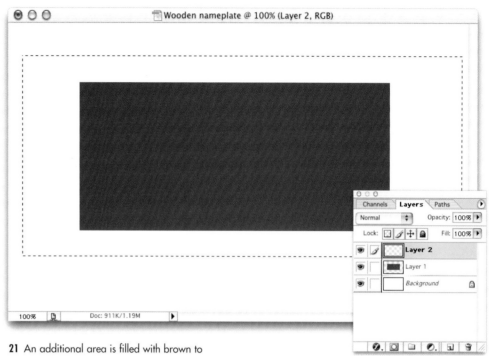

21 An additional area is filled with brown to serve as the basis for the texture.

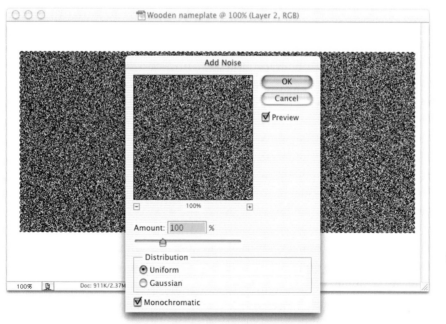

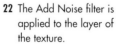

22 The Add Noise filter is applied to the layer of the texture.

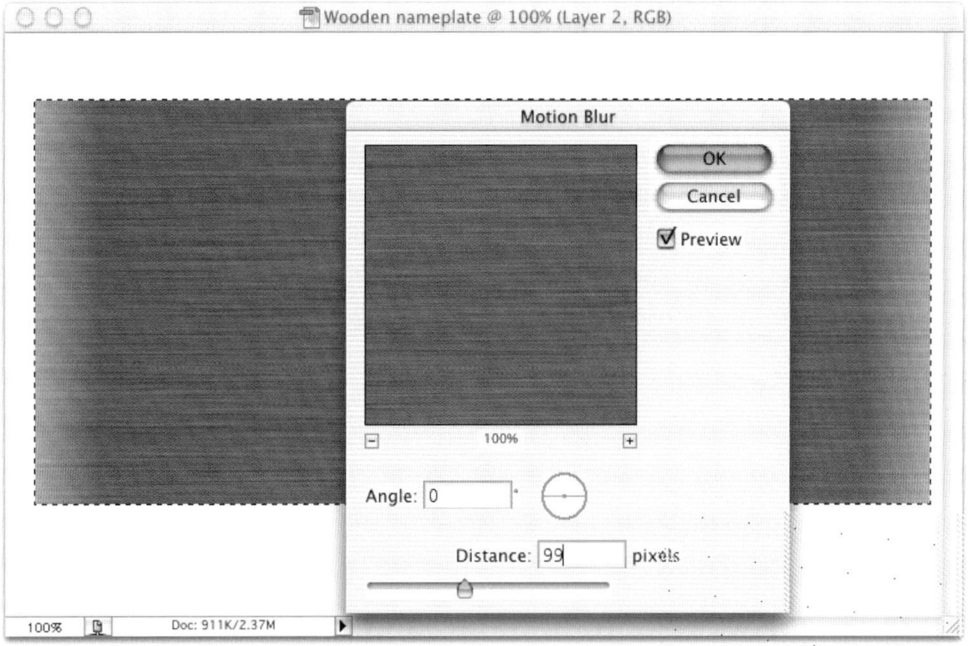

Next, you stretch the noise to get the look and feel of the wood's grain. Choose the Motion Blur filter (Filter>Blur>Motion Blur). With the Angle set to 0, move the Distance slider to a large number, such as 99 (Figure 23). Click OK.

Next, give the texture some contrast. Choose the Levels command (Image>Adjustments>Levels). Move the black and white triangles in to the center to darken your darks and lighten your lights. This gives the texture more detail (Figure 24). Click OK.

Now, you have a good wood grain texture that can be applied to any surface. Next, you warp the grain and add knotty areas.

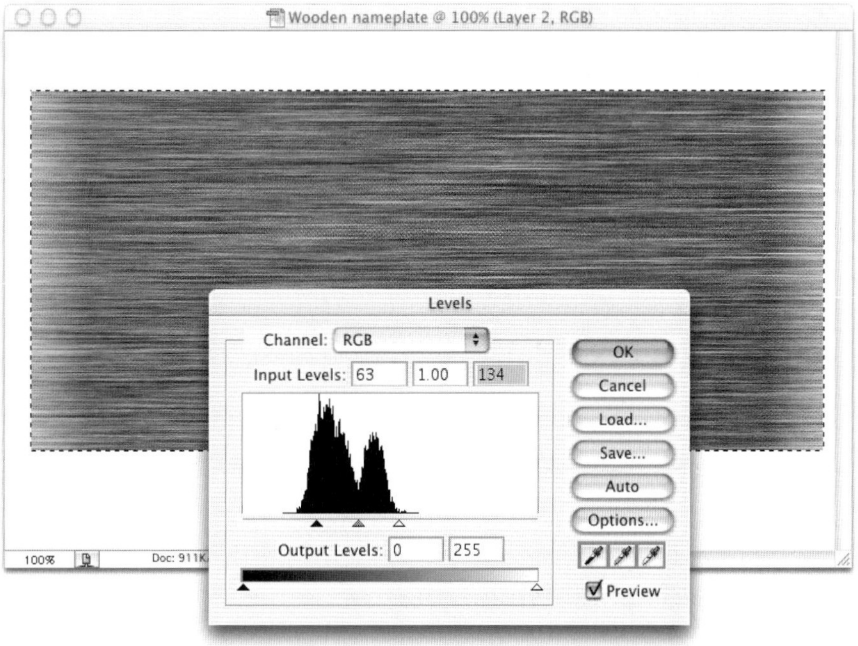

23 The Motion Blur filter is applied to the Texture layer.

24 With the Levels command, the contrast of the grain is increased.

Create a clipping group of the two layers by clicking between them in the Layers palette with the Option button (Alt on a PC) pressed. This uses the transparency information in the lower layer to mask out the part of the upper layer that has the grain (Figure 25).

Turn the lower layer into a selection by Command-clicking (Control-clicking on a PC) on it in the Layers palette. In the Liquify command (Filter>Liquify), select the Warp tool. Using a large-sized brush, run the tool over parts of the image to distort the grain. Experiment with a few different strokes. Follow the grain that is shown in Figure 26.

Switch to the Bloat tool, place it over an area where you want a knot to appear, and hold down the mouse button. This bloats the area (Figure 27). Click OK when you have achieved the desired effect. Deselect.

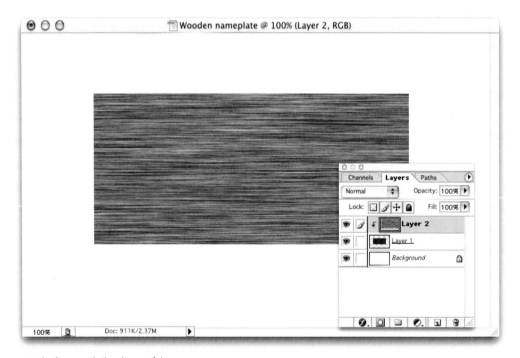

25 The layer with the shape of the wooden plate clips the layer with the wood grain texture.

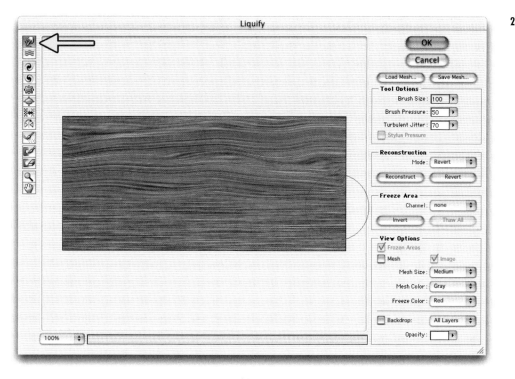

26 The Warp tool in the Liquify command is used to stretch out the grain.

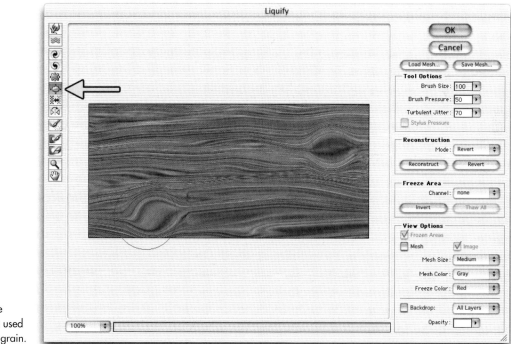

27 The Bloat tool in the Liquify command is used to add knots to the grain.

Click on the upper layer and choose Merge Down from the Layer's palette drop-down menu to merge the two layers into one (Figure 28). Double-click the merged layer to bring up the Layer Styles dialog box. Choose the Bevel and Emboss style. In the Structure section at the top of the dialog box, choose Chisel Hard for the Technique with a high value for the Depth option. The Depth value increases the lights and darks for the bevels. Crank up the size until the bevel is the size you want for the nameplate (Figure 29).

NOTE   Make sure that your document is visible behind the Layer Styles dialog box. It makes it easy to see the modifications you apply.

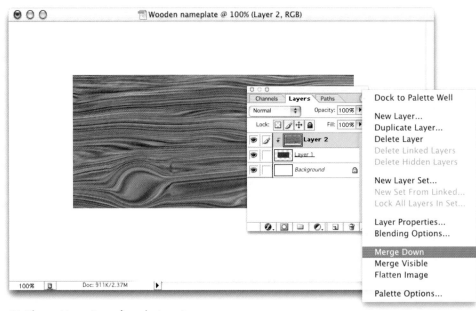

28 Choose Merge Down from the Layer's palette menu to merge the selected layer with the one under it.

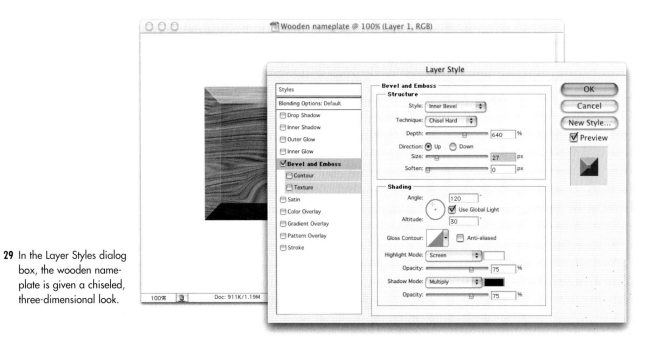

29 In the Layer Styles dialog box, the wooden nameplate is given a chiseled, three-dimensional look.

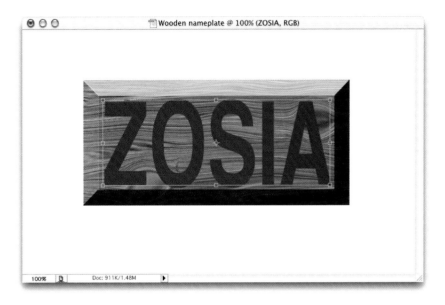

Finally, chisel a name into the wood. To do this, select the Text tool, choose an appropriate size and font, and then type in the name you want over the nameplate. Use the Scale function (Edit>Transform>Scale) to resize the text to fit within the boundaries of the interior of the wooden nameplate, as shown in Figure 30.

Because there will be an indentation in the wood, there should be an interruption that is visible in the grain. To achieve this effect, duplicate the layer of the wood and place the layer over the Text layer (Figure 31). Decrease the opacity slightly to show the letters underneath, making the wood grain inside the letter appear darker.

Clip a copy of the Wood layer with the Text layer. Move the duplicated Wood layer down slightly. Double-click the Text layer in the layer's palette to bring up the layer's styles, and choose Inner Shadow. Play with the size until you have created something that looks like a chiseled nameplate.

Press OK, and you are done (Figure 32).

30 The text created with the Text tool is scaled to fit within the area of the wooden nameplate.

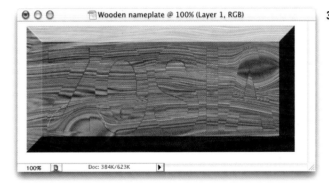

31 The Text layer is used to clip the duplicate of the wood. The duplicated Wood layer is moved down to break up the continuity of the wood grain.

32 The final result is a realistic looking wooden nameplate.

Weathered Wood

Figure 33 shows the "Bodega shadows" image. This was an experiment in creating wood patterns that captured the look of wood exposed to the ocean-side elements.

By eliminating the shadows and by zooming into an area of the deck, you can see different wood grain textures become visible. In Figure 34, the grains have more space between them, unlike the wood grain texture on the door of the Solano Grill.

33 "Bodega shadows" is an experiment in creating wood grains that are affected by weathering.

34 The grain in the wood is loosely spaced with specific shapes to the lines.

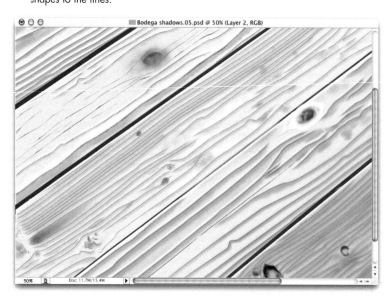

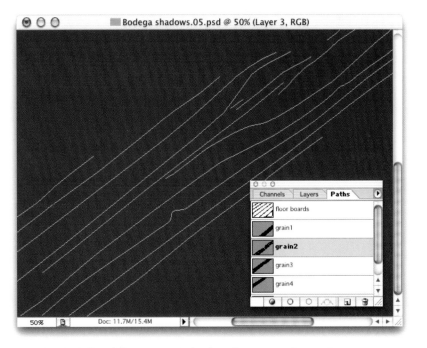

35 Using the Path tool, lines are created to form the grains in the wood.

The grain is nothing more than a series of paths that are created to simulate the lines that make up wood grains (Figure 35).

Each set of paths is divided into groups for the individual planks of wood on the deck.

A new layer is created for the wood grain and the paths are stroked with varying thicknesses of the Paintbrush tool, using a variety of colors to match real wood (Figure 36).

If you create wood textures, this procedure is enough. In this particular case, however, the wood is aged and weathered. This creates an effect where the grain lines are raised from the surface of the wood.

The layer that contains the stroked paths for the wood is duplicated by dragging it over the New Layer icon at the bottom of the Layer's palette (Figure 37).

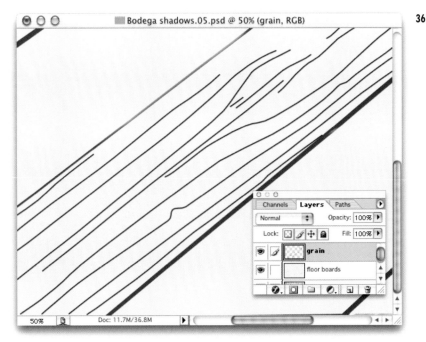

36 The paths are stroked with the Paintbrush tool.

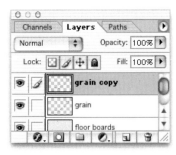

37 The layer with the stroked grain is duplicated.

38 The grain in the duplicated layer is motion blurred.

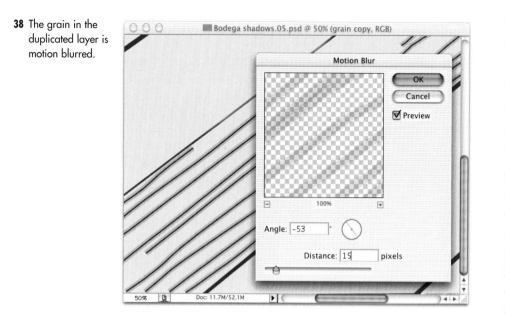

This new, duplicated layer is given a Motion Blur filter (Filter>Blur>Motion Blur) that has a direction that is perpendicular to the direction of the strokes (Figure 38).

Using the Move tool, the blurred layer was moved slightly down and away from the layer of the grain (Figure 39).

This blurred layer was then duplicated. With the transparency locked, it was filled with a white color. This layer was then moved up and away from the grain. The opacity was reduced in the two layers with the blurred lines. In Figure 40, you can see the effect. Note that a dark tone was added to the background to make the white stroke visible. The Add Noise filter was applied to the finished layer.

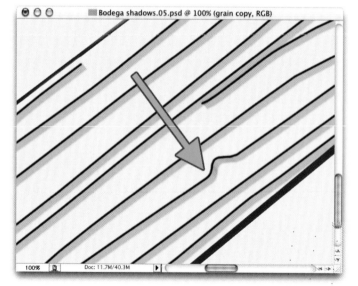

39 The blurred layer is moved and acts as an edge that is affected by light.

40 The two blurred layers act as the light and shadow caused by the raised grain.

Wood Bark on a Tree

Tree bark requires a different approach. Bark differs in texture and color from one type of tree to another. Certain types of bark are smooth and can be duplicated with a couple of filters, while other types have an intricate texture that require extra work.

The "Cedar" and "Solano Grill" images include trees that are large enough to see their bark texture (Figures 41 and 42). There is much similarity in the creation of the bark textures. The major difference is the use of color.

41 Details of the tree on the left side of the "Cedar" image.

42 Details of the tree that is positioned on the left side of the "Solano Grill" image.

In the "Cedar" image, I used a brown paintbrush to create the basic shape of the tree in its own layer. Then, I applied the Add Noise filter (Filter>Noise>Add Noise). This filter added a random texture that the next filter could expand on.

I used the Craquelure filter (Filter>Texture>Craquelure) to complete the basic bark texture (Figure 43). The Craquelure filter creates interesting textures that are manipulated to resemble soil, stone, or, in this case, tree bark. This texture appeared closer to the actual tree bark texture and provided a starting point from which to build the tree.

Additional texture was added with the Paintbrush tool by painting grooves into the bark.

Areas of the bark were selected with the Lasso tool. These areas were filled with an appropriate color to simulate damaged areas or bare parts of the bark (Figure 44). The Add Noise (Filter>Noise>Add Noise) filter was applied to these areas. For extra texture, dark grooves and shadows were added to the bark with the Paintbrush tool, using a soft edged brush tip and black for the color (Figure 45).

For the tree in the "Solano Grill" image, the Texturizer filter (Filter>Texture>Texturizer), in Sandstone mode, is substituted for the Craquelure filter. Different types of trees produce different types of bark. Which filter you choose depends on which one gives you the desired results. Photoshop comes with several filters, and you should experiment with them. Instead of using large damaged spots on the bark, such as the one in the previous tree example, small bumps are added to this tree, which is prevalent for the kind of tree it is. These bumps are simply dabs of light and dark tones that are created with the Paintbrush tool, as shown in Figure 46.

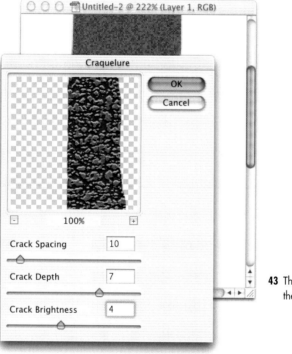

43 The Craquelure filter finalizes the basic bark texture.

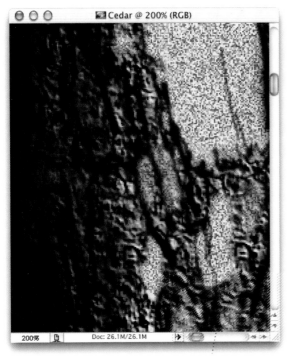

44 Selecting areas and filling them with color creates the damaged areas of the bark. Then, the areas are filtered with the Add Noise filter.

45 Using a soft-edged paintbrush, grooves and dark shadow areas are added to the bark.

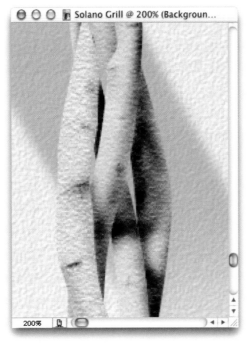

46 Small bumps are added to the bark with the Paintbrush tool.

Hard as a Rock

Stone. Now here is a study in variety! Is it marble, granite, or concrete? Is it polished or did it just arrive from the quarry? It helps to study reality in order to reproduce it. I cannot stress this enough.

Color and texture are the most important considerations for determining the material that makes up an object. Consider the "KCC" painting that is shown in Figure 47. Note that the stone façade is painted with bright colors. In this case, it is primarily the texture that determines the look of the façade material.

47 The "KCC" painting shows a brightly painted building with a stucco façade.

48 The basic shapes of the wall are laid out with the Pen tool.

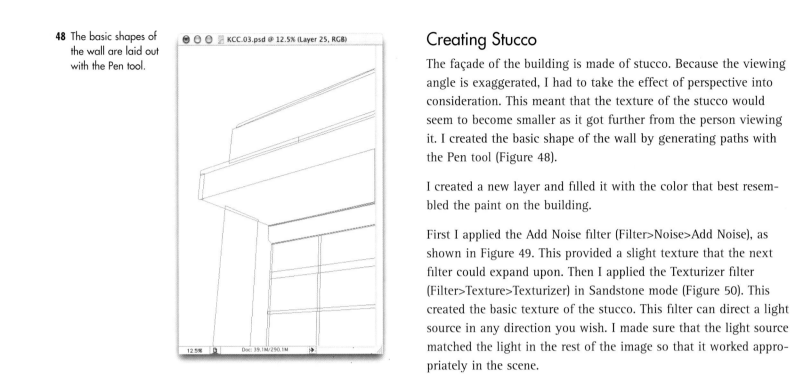

Creating Stucco

The façade of the building is made of stucco. Because the viewing angle is exaggerated, I had to take the effect of perspective into consideration. This meant that the texture of the stucco would seem to become smaller as it got further from the person viewing it. I created the basic shape of the wall by generating paths with the Pen tool (Figure 48).

I created a new layer and filled it with the color that best resembled the paint on the building.

First I applied the Add Noise filter (Filter>Noise>Add Noise), as shown in Figure 49. This provided a slight texture that the next filter could expand upon. Then I applied the Texturizer filter (Filter>Texture>Texturizer) in Sandstone mode (Figure 50). This created the basic texture of the stucco. This filter can direct a light source in any direction you wish. I made sure that the light source matched the light in the rest of the image so that it worked appropriately in the scene.

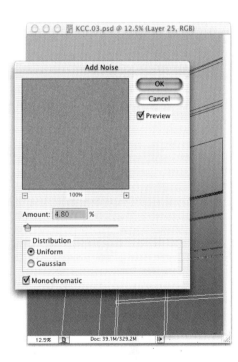

49 The Add Noise filter is applied to the layer that is filled with the color for the walls.

50 The Texturizer filter is applied to the layer finalizing the texture.

The layer was then distorted (Edit>Transform>Distort) so that the top or further-most section narrowed from the bottom. This compressed the texture at the narrow end, which created the illusion that it is smaller on top (Figure 51). Because it is farther away from your point of view, this is how it should appear.

To add additional texture and the look of roughness to the wall, I used the Lasso tool with a feathered edge to select random areas of the wall, and then applied the Texturizer filter at the same setting (Figure 52). Feathering the selection allowed the new filter application to blend in smoothly to the surrounding area.

The edge of the wall required irregularities to complete the effect of a rough texture. These were accomplished using a paintbrush to add little dark areas with light dabs underneath the areas. The direction of the light source dictated the placement of the lights and darks (Figure 53). Because the light was coming from above, placing the dark tones at the top of the intended blemish makes it look like an indent in the surface. Reversing the lights and darks makes it look like a bump that extends out from the surface. This concept is explored in more detail in Chapter 4, "Lights and Shadows."

Close examination of most of my California paintings reveals that I use this technique often. I live in the Bay Area, and it just so happens that stucco is a preferred material for construction.

51 The colored, textured layer is distorted to follow the perspective of the building.

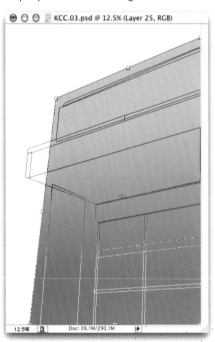

52 Random areas are selected with a feathered lasso and subjected to the Texturizer filter.

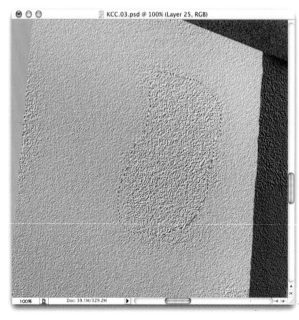

53 Depending on the direction of the light source, the placement of highlights and shadows determines whether a surface blemish appears raised or indented.

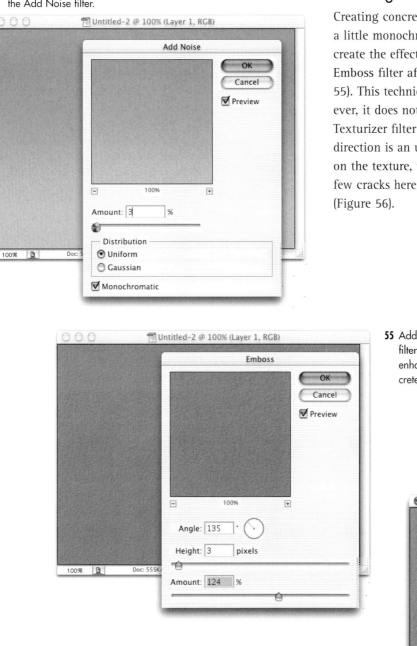

54 Concrete is achieved with the Add Noise filter.

Creating Concrete

Creating concrete is a simpler process. In many cases, adding just a little monochromatic noise to a gray-colored shape is enough to create the effect. To achieve slightly more texture, apply the Emboss filter after you apply the Add Noise filter (Figures 54 and 55). This technique is similar in result to the Texturizer filter; however, it does not utilize the light source direction control that the Texturizer filter provides. If you create a sidewalk, the light source direction is an unwanted effect, as there is too much emphasis on the texture, which makes it look rougher than it should. A few cracks here and there increase the realism of the texture (Figure 56).

55 Adding the Emboss filter to the noise enhances the concrete look.

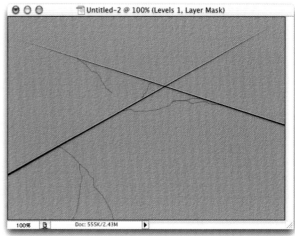

56 The sidewalk shows the Add Noise/Emboss combination with a few cracks added for realism.

As Thick as a Brick

A brick wall is a collection of small rectangular stone-textured shapes, which are fairly symmetrical in placement. The best way to achieve the effect of a brick wall is to create the shape for the wall and fill it with a pattern. Little modification adds a sense of randomness to the bricks.

Creating the basic pattern is a simple procedure. Let's create this image together.

In Photoshop, create a new document that measures about 10 by 10 inches. Set the resolution to 72 dpi, as shown in Figure 57.

NOTE   The parameters for the new document make the file small enough for things to work fast on any machine. This is only an exercise and not intended for reproduction. If you have a fast machine, you can work on a larger file.

Make the grid visible by choosing Show Grid under the View menu (View>Show>Grid) (Figure 58). Go to the Preferences dialog box for the Grid (For a Mac OS 9.1 or later, choose Edit> Preferences>Guides, Grid & Slices, and for Mac OS X, choose Photoshop>Preferences>Guides, Grid & Slices). Set the Grid Subdivisions to 11, as shown in Figure 59.

57 The parameters are set for a new file where the brick wall is created.

58 Show Grid is chosen to view the grid over the canvas.

NOTE In order to make the creation and selection processes easier, I changed the grid subdivisions in the Preferences dialog box to an uneven number. The odd-numbered square in the grid creates the space necessary for the grout between the bricks.

Create a new layer. Zoom in so that one grid section takes up the entire screen. This makes it easier to see what you are doing.

With the Rectangle selection tool, select a rectangular shape that takes up 4 subdivisions down and 11 across.

Fill the selection with a color similar to that of a brick (Figure 60).

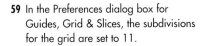

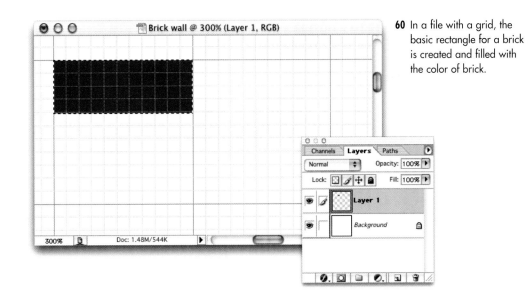

59 In the Preferences dialog box for Guides, Grid & Slices, the subdivisions for the grid are set to 11.

60 In a file with a grid, the basic rectangle for a brick is created and filled with the color of brick.

Clone the brick over to the right and down to form the pattern (Figure 61). Make sure that the space between each brick is a one-grid subdivision. Place the brick in the second row so that the brick is set with the odd subdivision for the brick above it to serve as the vertical grout space.

Make sure the background is transparent by clicking off the Eye icon in the Background layer. Now, return to the top layer and with the Rectangular Marquee tool, the bricks are selected (Figure 62) and turned into a pattern by selecting the Define Pattern option in the Edit menu (Edit>Define Pattern) (Figure 63). Note the specific area that is selected in Figure 62. This ensures that the pattern is accurate. The excess grid area selected on the left and under the brick at the bottom of the grid creates the grout area on the opposite side of the brick. Where one edge of the pattern ends, the other one picks up. This is called step and repeat.

After the pattern is created, deselect the areas (choose Command-D on a Mac or Control-D on a PC).

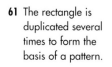

61 The rectangle is duplicated several times to form the basis of a pattern.

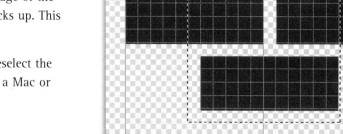
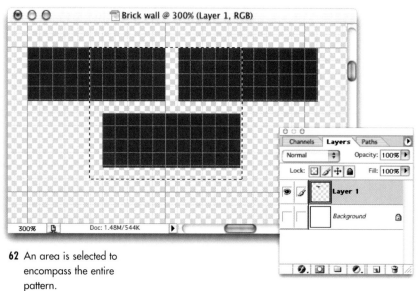

62 An area is selected to encompass the entire pattern.

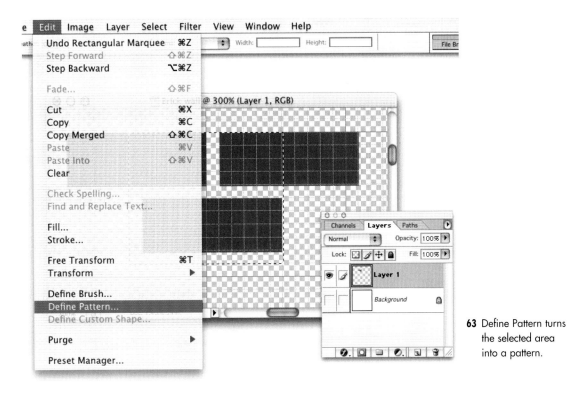

63 Define Pattern turns
the selected area
into a pattern.

64 A dialog box appears
where you can name
the pattern.

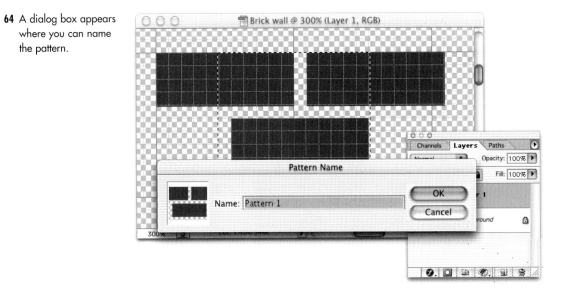

Zoom back to a 100% view and turn off the Eye icon for the layer where you created the pattern. Turn on the Eye icon for the Background layer.

Create a new layer and fill it with the pattern of bricks. To do this, press Shift-Delete or choose Fill from the Edit menu. In the Use section of the dialog box, choose Pattern, and in the Custom Pattern window, select the bricks pattern (Figure 65).

A layer for the wall is created behind the area with the bricks. This layer is filled with the color you want the grout to be (Figure 66). The Add Noise filter is applied in Monochrome mode with an amount that is adequate to simulate the rough quality of grout.

Now you need to add texture to the bricks. The Add Noise filter does the trick (Figure 67). The amount of noise added should be less than the amount added to the grout.

65 In the Fill command dialog box, choose the pattern.

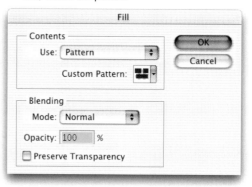

66 The layer is filled with the color you want the grout to be, and the Add Noise filter is applied.

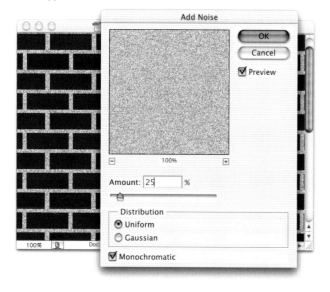

67 The Add Noise filter is applied to the brick pattern to give it texture.

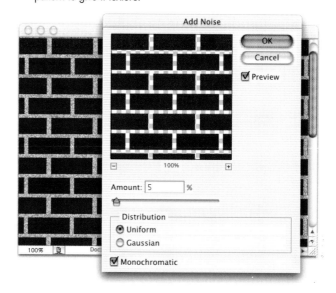

Select the layer with the brick pattern. Double-click on it in the Layer's palette to bring up its Layer Style. Apply the Bevel and Emboss layer style (Figure 68). Choose Outer Bevel for the Style. This adds dimension to the bricks, and it makes them look as if they are protruding from the wall.

Finally, you must achieve the random nature of a brick wall. With the Dodge and Burn tools, dab random bricks with the brush set to the size of the height of a brick. You randomly darken and lighten individual bricks to give the wall a more realistic look (Figure 69).

Adding an occasional crack here and there adds even more realism. Use a tiny paintbrush set to a dark color to create little cracks. For an added wear and tear effect, use a small Eraser tool and hit the edges of the bricks to remove the hard edges.

68 The Bevel and Emboss layer style effect is applied to the layer of the brick pattern.

69 A zoomed-in view of the wall shows individual bricks that are altered with the Dodge and Burn tools to create a more weathered appearance and cracks.

Heavy Metal

Metal, like wood and stone, comes in a variety of different looks. Gold, for example, is shiny and yellow. Iron is dull and black, and it has a little rust on it. Metal also has a textured surface.

Basic metal textures are fairly easy to create. Like the procedures for other materials, you must first create the metallic shape or object. I usually do this with the Pen tool. Then, you decide what metal you are going to create. This determines the color, though this is not crucial. Because most shiny metals have a uniform surface, using the Hue/Saturation command (Image> Adjust>Hue/Saturation) allows you to quickly change the color. You can play alchemist and amaze your friends by turning tin into gold right before their eyes.

The image in Figure 70 is called "red doors." Catchy huh? If you look closer at the hardware on the doors, you see that they look like metal. Sure, doorknobs are usually metal, but this is not always the case. These are metal, as shown in Figure 71. How can you tell? You can tell by the way they are rendered.

Paths are created with the Pen tool for each part of the hardware in addition to the reflections cast on them (Figure 72).

Each individual path is turned into a selection and filled with a corresponding color. Figure 73 shows the path for the base plate selected and filled with a Radial gradient. I used a light brown for the Foreground color and a dark brown for the Background color. I clicked at the point where I wanted the highlight (light brown) and dragged outward to the edge of the selected area.

70 The "red doors" image.

71 A close look at the hardware on the doors reveals that the material they are made of is metal.

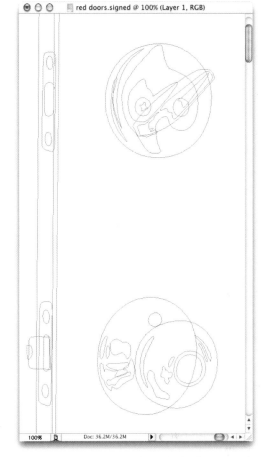

72 The paths for the pieces of hardware in addition to the shapes for the reflections are created.

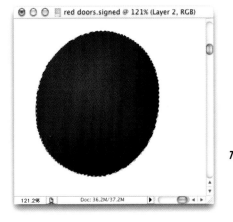

73 The path for the plate that fastens the knob to the door is selected and filled with a gradient.

I Applied a drop shadow in the Layer Style dialog box for the layer containing the plate (Figure 74). The Angle option was set to simulate light coming from below because the strongest light in this image source is the sunlight cascading across the floor from outside the doorway. Note that the Use Global Light option is checked. This ensures that any drop shadows applied to other layers are lit in the same way.

In another layer, two of the paths that make up highlights are turned into selections (Figure 75). The reflections of lit objects in the room cast multi-colored shapes on the metal of the plate. To achieve this effect, I expanded the selection (Select>Modify> Expand) and feathered (Select>Feather) to soften the glow (Figures 76 and 77). Then I filled it with the desired color. In this case, it was filled with a red-colored tint, as shown in Figure 78.

This process is repeated; however, for the second time, it was given less of an expand and feather and filled with a yellow. The third and final selection is not expanded, but it is feathered and filled with a white color (Figure 79).

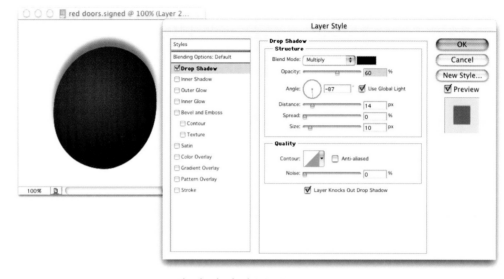

74 The doorknob plate is given a drop shadow in the Layer Style dialog box.

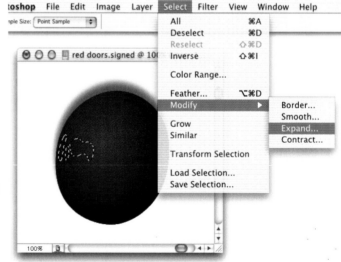

75 The path is turned into a selection, and Expand is chosen from the Modify menu.

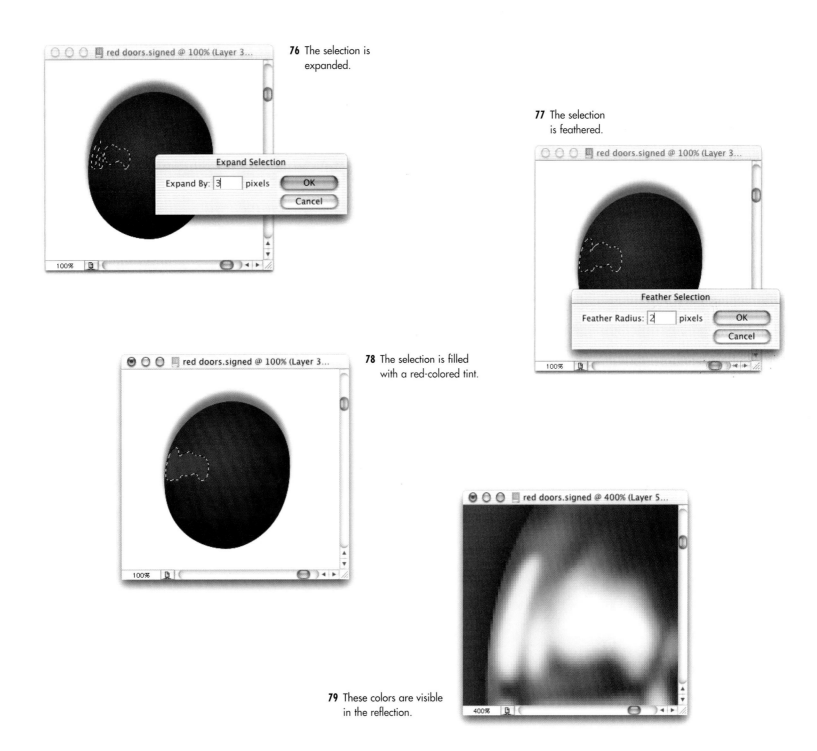

76 The selection is expanded.

Expand Selection

Expand By: 3 pixels

OK

Cancel

100%

77 The selection is feathered.

Feather Selection

Feather Radius: 2 pixels

OK

Cancel

100%

78 The selection is filled with a red-colored tint.

100%

79 These colors are visible in the reflection.

400%

The other tones visible in the plate were achieved in a similar manner. Some areas needed an additional adjustment, such as the ones shown in Figure 80. I used the Smudge tool to give these a little tug.

Figure 81 shows another image in which I used this technique. The use of a different set of colors gives you a different type of metal.

Reflections are crucial in creating the illusion of a polished metallic material. Such a metal reflects the surrounding environment and other objects near it. Chapter 7, "Reflections," expands on this concept.

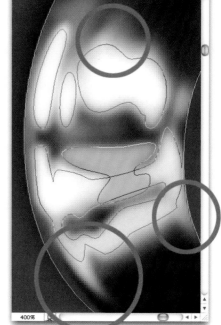

80 These areas are modified with the Smudge Tool.

81 The "handles" image shows the same technique; however, the type of metal appears different because of the varying colors used.

The Best for Last

Photoshop 7 introduces a new way to create textures. It is called *Pattern Maker*. This feature is found next to Liquify and Extract, which are located under the Filter menu (Figure 82). This new feature does not replace the old Define Pattern function. It is simply a new approach to the concept of creating textures in Photoshop. Though the name Pattern Maker is a bit misleading, you will see that random textures are what this baby is really meant for.

At first sight you can see that the Pattern Maker dialog box is a close relative to the Extract dialog box and the Liquify dialog box, as shown in Figure 83.

When you enter the Pattern Maker function, you see your image in the view box. Here you can specify the area in your image where you want to create the texture. The texture is created based on the elements in that selection. In Figure 83, you can see on the upper-left portion of the dialog box, there is a Marquee tool. In Figure 84, I selected a small area of the image.

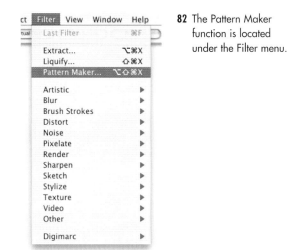

82 The Pattern Maker function is located under the Filter menu.

83 The dialog box for the Pattern Maker has a multitude of controls for creating textures.

84 Using the Pattern Maker's rectangular selection tool, a small section of the image is selected.

Setting the Width and Height to equal numbers in the Generation section in the dialog box produces a noticeable pattern that tiles (Figure 85). The tiles are the size you input for the width and height.

Entering unequal numbers produces various interesting distortions. Figure 86 shows a higher number setting for the Height. This results in an elongated pattern of long, vertical lines.

You can also offset the patterns to create brick-type patterns. Use the Offset button to select which direction you want for the offset. Figure 87 shows a square pattern tile that is offset on the vertical. Figure 88 shows the offset on the horizontal.

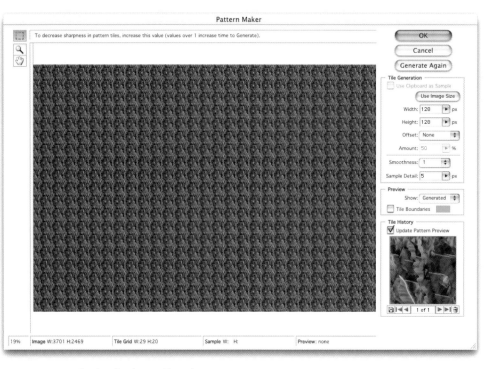

85 Entering equal values for the Width and Height options produces a tiled pattern.

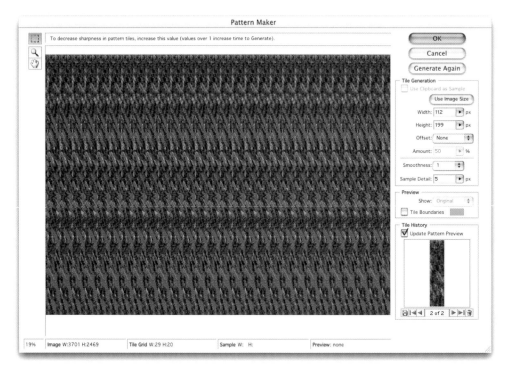

86 Entering unequal amounts for either the Width or the Height will produces asymmetrical tiled patterns.

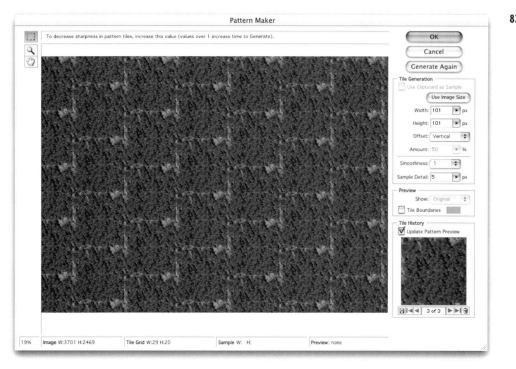

87 An equal-sided shape with a vertical offset forms a brick pattern.

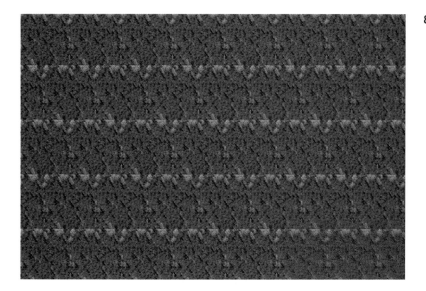

88 The same equal-sided shape with a horizontal offset in the opposite direction.

The Use Image Size button is the one I like. It generates a pattern equal to the dimensions of the image itself, as shown in Figure 89. This creates a texture that has no noticeable pattern. Playing with this feature can result in some stunning results.

In Figure 90, I cranked up the Sample Detail. This gave me a lush texture that looks like fabric. Keep in mind that the textures came from the same sampled area shown in Figure 84.

NOTE As you are experimenting, the Tile History feature, located at the bottom-right side of the dialog box, keeps a record of your alterations. This makes it easier to go back and forth between your patterns.

The possibilities are endless. What Photoshop introduces here is a whole new way to doodle.

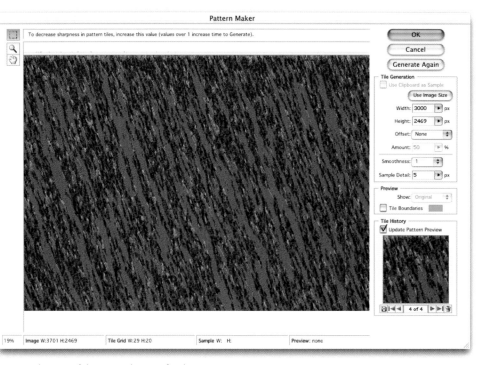

89 Use the size of the original image for the pattern to create a random looking texture.

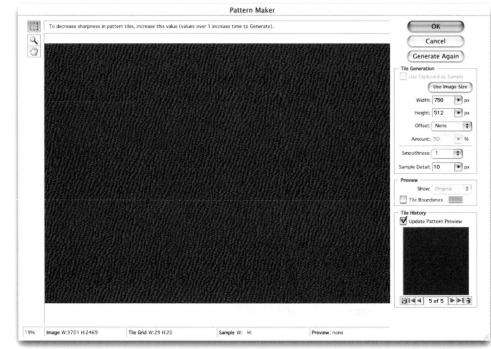

90 Increasing the level of detail gives you a stronger texture.

6

Creating the Elements

A Rainy Day

Rain, snow, fire, smoke, water, fog—sounds like the inventory list for a meteorologist. Each of these elements can easily take center stage in an image. Rain is used to set a mood. Many sad scenes use rain as a focal point. What is the Christmas holiday without snow? Smoke and fire can identify a cozy camping scene or a horrific disaster. They can also signify the exhaust from a rocket to Mars.

Regardless of the situation, these elements set mood. The Layer Styles tool makes creating these effects a relatively simple procedure. The Liquify feature takes care of some of the other effects, and a few filters and layer tricks take care of the rest.

This chapter starts by discussing rain, which is depicted in many forms. It can represent a torrential downpour or a light sun shower. The overall lighting of a scene should correspond to the amount of rainfall depicted.

Figure 1 shows the lake in Central Park that I took on a recent trip back to my old hometown. It is a clear, cold February afternoon. In this chapter, we are going to change the weather and make it a gloomy, rainy day. As noted previously, the lighting is crucial for setting the mood.

First, I separated the buildings from the sky. This is necessary to apply effects to the sky area while leaving the rest of the image unaffected. The Color Range selection method is not as practical in this instance because there is an overall blue cast to the image. In this case, selecting the sky takes in too much of the rest of the image. I made an alpha channel mask to do the trick.

NOTE Using an alpha channel was the best method for this particular image. Other images may require a different form for selection. For example, if the color of the sky is different or separated sufficiently from the rest of the image, the Magic Wand tool might be the only tool you need to use.

I determined which of the three color channels gave me the best contrast. Figure 2 is the red channel, Figure 3 is the green channel, and Figure 4 is the blue channel. The blue channel is the best choice in this case. In Figure 4, you can see how well delineated the sky is from the rest of the image. Next, I duplicated the blue channel into an alpha channel by dragging it over the New Channel icon at the bottom of the Channel's palette.

1 This image of Central Park in New York City was taken with a Nikon CoolPix 995.

In the alpha channel, I used the Invert command (Image>Adjustments>Invert) to turn the channel into a negative (Figure 5). This creates an effective visual separation of the tones that need to be modified. I used the Curves command in Arbitrary mode (Figure 6) to set the gray values that force the foreground to white, as shown in Figure 7.

2 The red channel.

3 The green channel.

4 The blue channel.

5 The alpha channel is inverted to a negative, so that you can clearly see the tones in the buildings.

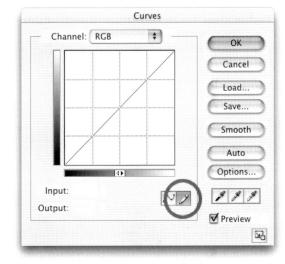

6 The Curves command in Arbitrary mode.

7 The Curves command forces the tones of the buildings to turn white.

With a white Paintbrush, any unwanted artifacts left behind are removed, such as windows, and so on. The alpha channel is then inverted again. This leaves a mask for the sky area, as seen in Figure 8.

Now begins the alteration of the scene to set the mood for a stormy day—with clouds. You can't have rain without clouds. The alpha channel is turned into a selection by Command-clicking (Control-clicking on a PC) on it in the channel's palette. I chose Inverse (Select>Inverse) to select the buildings. I then sent the buildings to their own layer (Layer>New>Layer Via Copy).

Next, I created a new layer behind the layer of the buildings to house the clouds. I chose a foreground color that simulates dark storm clouds. I also chose a color for the background to simulate the sky (Figure 9). I applied the Clouds filter (Filter>Render>Clouds), creating a cloudbank that is visible behind the buildings, as shown in Figure 10.

8 The alpha channel is inverted to create a mask for the sky.

9 Colors are chosen to simulate a stormy sky.

10 Stormy clouds replace the sky.

The clouds actually extend over the entire image area, although you can't see all of them because the Building layer blocks them. I produced smaller, concentrated, and more believable clouds by scaling this layer down (Edit>Transform>Scale) until it barely fit the area that was going to be visible (Figure 11).

With a large, soft-edged paintbrush, I modified the clouds using the two colors they were created with to add and subtract clouds (Figure 12).

11 The layer with the clouds is scaled down to concentrate it into the visible sky area.

12 Using a large, soft-edged brush, the clouds are modified.

Next, I needed to change the overall lighting to set the mood. After the storm clouds are added, it makes no visual sense for the buildings to appear as sunny as they are in the original. Therefore, the layer with the buildings is selected as the active layer. A New Adjustment layer is created and set to Hue/Saturation. I selected the Group With Previous Layer option (Figure 13). Adjustments now only affect the layer with the buildings.

The Saturation and the Lightness settings are lowered to a level that best simulates the look the city would have under rainy conditions, as shown in Figure 14.

13 The Group With Previous Layer option is selected in the Adjustment Layer dialog box.

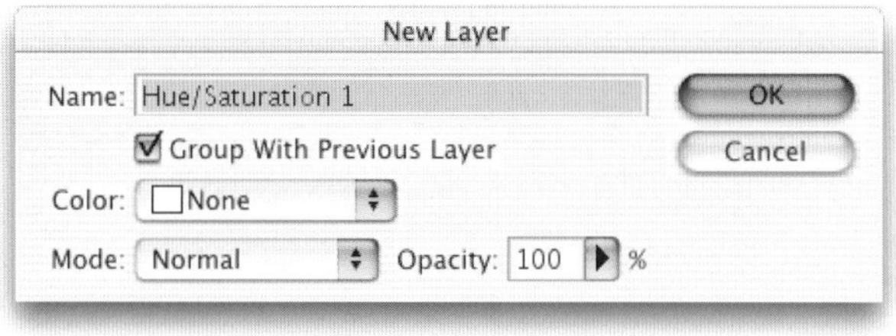

14 The layer of the buildings is adjusted to simulate stormy conditions.

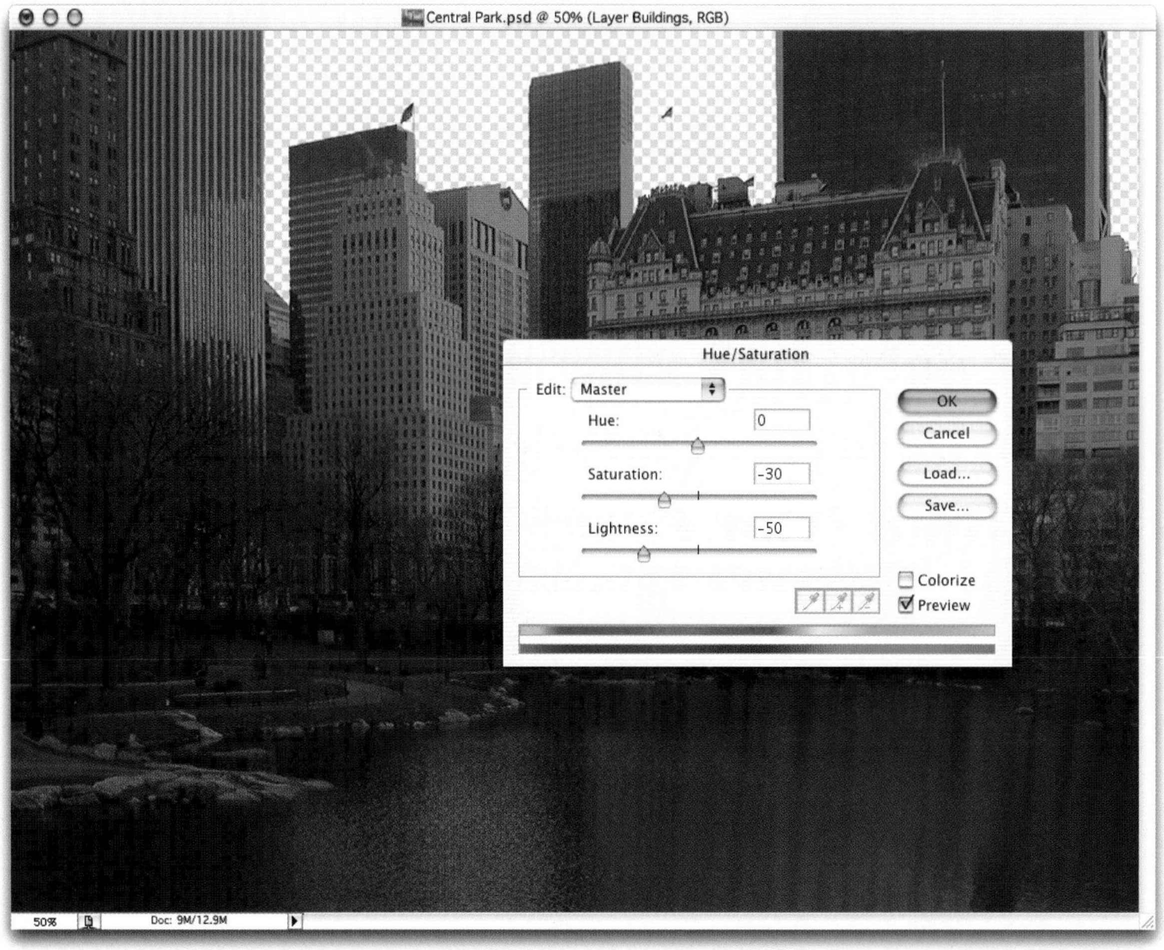

15 Noise is added to the black-filled layer.

Now, it's time to create the downpour! The mood is created. The image just needs some falling rain. A new layer is created above the other layers, and it's filled with black. The Add Noise filter is applied at a high percentage (Filter>Noise>Add Noise). The Distribution option is set to Gaussian. The Monochromatic option is also selected to ensure that no other colors are introduced (Figure 15).

NOTE Uniform noise gets its name because the pixels it throws into the picture are distributed uniformly over the range of lightness that the Amount setting governs. In the settings shown in Figure 15, before the noise is added, the pixels are at 100%. After the filter is applied, most of the pixels are still at 100%; however, the ones that have changed can be as light as approximately 40%. These changed pixels are as likely to be 40% as they are to be 52%, or 73%, or 87%. Gaussian noise, on the other hand, tapers the distribution of the changed pixels. The same amount of pixels change, but with Gaussian noise, they are more likely to be 95% versus 90%, and far more likely to be 95% versus 40%. In addition, the taper continues well beyond the range of Uniform noise. A significant number of pixels might reach 10%, or they might even become pure white.

16 A Gaussian Blur is applied to the noise.

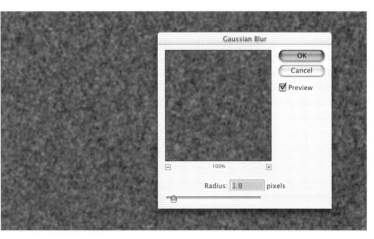

The Gaussian blur filter is used (Filter>Blur>Gaussian Blur) to soften the layer of the noise (Figure 16).

The Levels command (Image>Adjustments> Levels) gives the noise more contrast and separation (Figure 17).

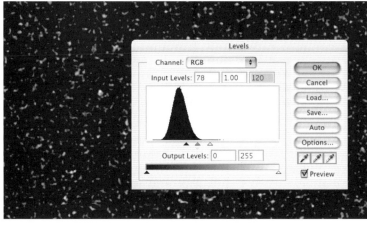

17 The Levels command is used to increase the contrast for the blurred noise.

The layer with the blurred noise is then put in Screen mode. In Screen mode, areas that are black in the top layer don't change the bottom layer. Lighter areas, however, lighten the underlying image and can create the streaks of rain that I wanted to produce for this image.

The Final touch is to make the rain appear as if it is falling down. This is accomplished with the Motion Blur filter (Filter>Blur>Motion Blur). The angle is set to the direction the rain will be falling. The Distance option is set high enough to stretch the white shapes long enough to simulate rain (Figure 18). The final result is visible in Figure 19.

18 The noise is streaked with the Motion Blur filter.

19 The result is a believable, rainy scene.

Standing Water

After the rain stops, if you take a closer look at the aftermath, you might see puddles on the sidewalk. Creating this effect is an interesting challenge and requires a different set of techniques than the ones used to create the rain.

First, you must create the sidewalk. Create a new file and fill it with a gradient of light gray at the bottom to a darker gray at the top, as shown in Figure 20. This light to dark transition helps to give the illusion of depth. Using the Pen tool, create a couple of lines to represent the divisions in the pavement (Figure 21). I used the Pen tool to create the lines because I did not want to create straight lines. Notice that the lines get thinner as they recede toward the back. This is to achieve the proper perspective, as discussed in Chapter 1, "Off to a Good Start." A slight, white edge is added to emphasize depth and the effect the light has on the indents in the pavement. I gave the lines' layer a Bevel and Emboss Layer Style. Try variations of Layer Styles on your own to see the different results.

Use the Paintbrush tool in Normal mode with black and use two small brush sizes (1 and 3) to create small cracks in the sidewalk (Figure 22).

Because the computer-generated gradient is too perfect to represent realistic looking cement, the Add Noise filter is applied (Filter>Noise>Add Noise). Just enough noise is used to add some texture, as seen in Figure 23.

NOTE   The real purpose of the noise is to provide randomized texture for the next filter you add.

20 A gray gradient is applied.

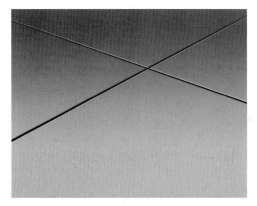

21 Lines are created to represent the slabs in the sidewalk.

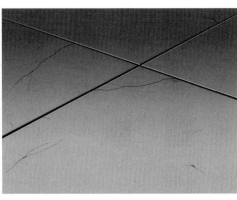

22 Cracks are added to the pavement.

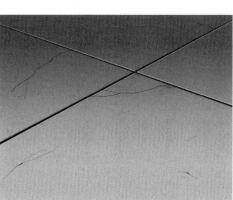

23 The Add Noise filter is used to add texture to the pavement.

The Plastic Wrap filter (Filter>Artistic>Plastic Wrap), shown in Figure 24 and Figure 25, used next creates the illusion of a wet sidewalk. This filter creates a sheen effect on a surface, as if you stretched plastic wrap over it. The added noise to the image increases the amount of shiny bumps that are added to the sidewalk (Figure 26).

Because the pavement is wet, it should be reflective. Figure 27 shows the image that is used for the reflection. This type of perspective is necessary for making the reflection look appropriate.

After importing the reflection image into the file of the sidewalk, it is rotated 180 degrees so that it appears upside down, like a reflection. It is then filtered with the Ripple filter (Filter>Distort>Ripple), which is shown in Figures 28 and 29. The result is shown in Figure 30.

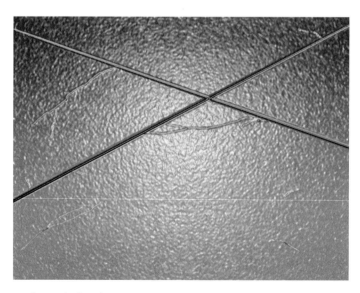

24 The Plastic Wrap filter.

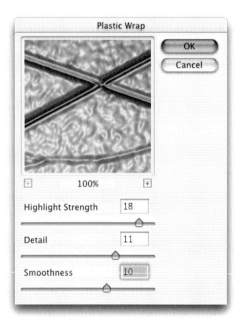

25 The dialog box for the Plastic Wrap filter.

26 The result of applying the Plastic Wrap filter to the pavement.

27 This image serves as a reflection, as it has the correct perspective—one that looks up at the buildings.

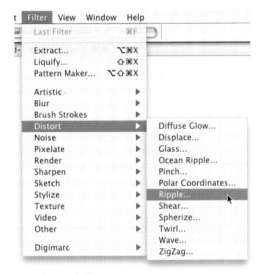

28 The Ripple filter.

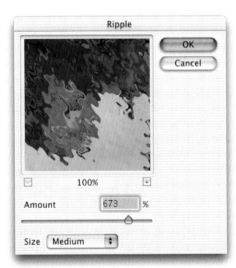

29 The dialog box for the Ripple filter.

30 The result of the Ripple filter on the rotated image.

The mode for the layer of the reflection is changed to Overlay mode, and the opacity is decreased enough to make the sidewalk visible (Figure 31).

NOTE   You should experiment with the mode settings to achieve the best results for your images.

A final touch is added to the image to make it look like stray drops of water are falling from above. Using the Elliptical Marquee tool, small ellipses are selected. With a small paintbrush, small dabs of color are then added to the selected area. The colors for the dabs are the lightest and darkest tones from the image (Figure 32). They are randomly placed for the purpose of the next filter used–the ZigZag filter.

The ZigZag filter is applied (Filter>Distort> ZigZag) next (Figure 33). This filter creates pond ripples (Figure 34). I used the ZigZag filter to create stray drops of water in a few other areas. This completes the scene, as shown in Figure 35.

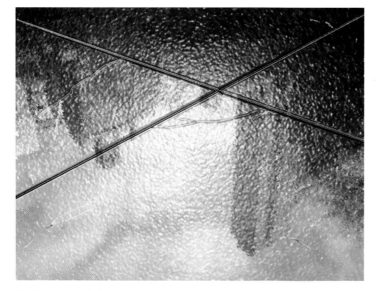

31 The layer with the reflection is set to Overlay mode, and its opacity is reduced.

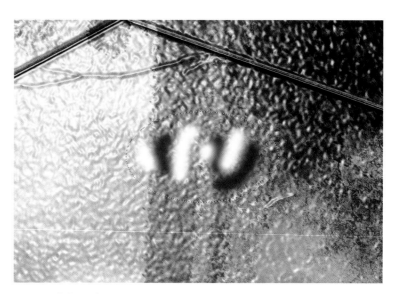

32 A small elliptical area is selected. Strokes of light and dark tones are added to give the image color.

33 The ZigZag filter.

34 The dialog box for the ZigZag filter.

35 The final image of the puddle on a sidewalk.

A Drop in the Bucket

Recently, I was commissioned to create a cold, frosty can of soda dripping with water as if it had just come out of an ice chest. It was for a poster on conservation. There had to be several drops of water on the can to make it look realistic. I was not prepared to illustrate hundreds of drops of water. Layer Styles makes this job easy.

I started the project by throwing some water onto a smooth surface and studying the effects of the droplets. As I mentioned previously, the study of reality is the best way to re-create it effectively.

Let's try this project together. Create a file that has a lined texture, like the one shown in Figure 36. The technique works over any image. I chose a lined texture because there is an effect discussed later that is best demonstrated over a texture of this type.

Create a new layer. In this new layer, use the paintbrush to create the shapes you want to appear, and create them as if they are made out of water. I chose to write out the word wet, as seen in Figure 37.

Double-click on the layer in the Layer's palette. The Layer Style dialog box appears. This is where the entire effect is created. The dialog box also gives you a preview of the effects while they are being created.

36 A background with a blue gradient and thin, horizontal line patter is created.

37 Use a white paintbrush to paint the word wet onto a blank layer.

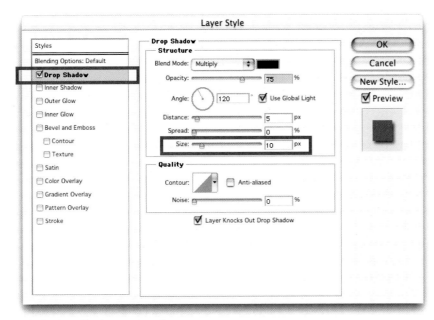

Choose the Drop Shadow option and increase the Size option to approximately 10 px (Figure 38).

Next, choose the Inner Shadow option. Choose Overlay for the Blend Mode, and increase the Opacity setting to 100% (Figure 39).

38 The Drop Shadow portion of the Layer Style dialog box.

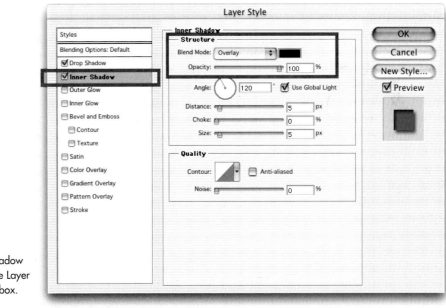

39 The Inner Shadow portion of the Layer Style dialog box.

Next, choose the Bevel and Emboss option.
Choose Chisel Hard for the Technique setting
(Figure 40).

Set the Depth field to a high percentage. I set it
to 540%. This increases the intensity of the
light and shadow on the bevel. Set the Soften
field to approximately 11 px (Figure 41).

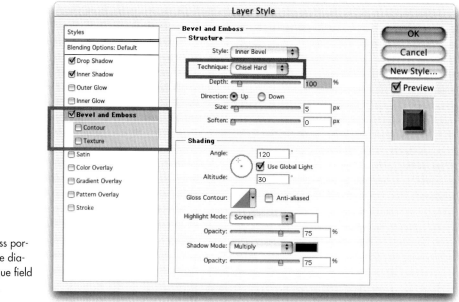

40 The Bevel and Emboss portion of the Layer Style dialog box. The Technique field
is set to Chisel Hard.

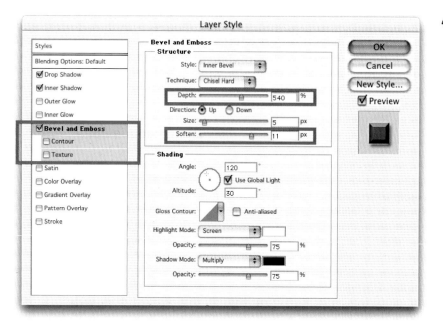

41 The Bevel and Emboss portion of the Layer Style dialog box. The Depth field is
set to a high percentage.

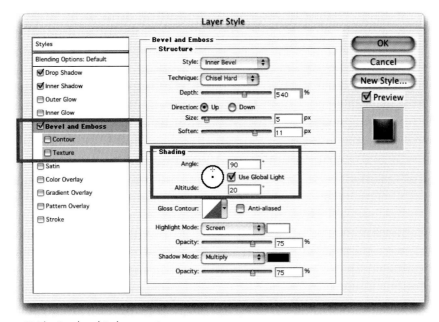

Set the Shading section's Angle field to 90 degrees, and set the Altitude to 20 degrees (Figure 42).

Set the Highlight Mode field to Screen, and the Opacity to 100%. Set the Shadow Mode field to Color Dodge with an Opacity value of 50% (Figure 43).

42 The Bevel and Emboss portion of the Layer Style dialog box. The attributes for the Shading section are set.

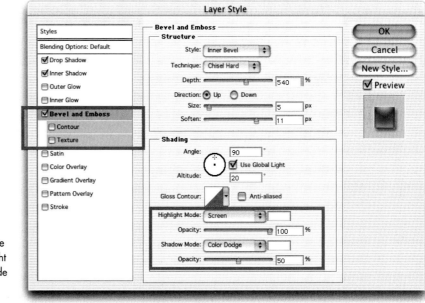

43 The Bevel and Emboss portion of the Layer Style dialog box. The Highlight Mode and Shadow Mode are set.

The next step in the Layer Style dialog box completes the effect. Choose the Blending Options option, as seen in Figure 44. Set the Fill Opacity field of the Advanced Blending section to 0%. This causes the active pixels in the layer (which are the white letters) to disappear, while leaving all the layer styles visible.

Click OK to exit the dialog box. The liquid should look realistic. One additional effect is needed to complete the image. Note that water acts like a magnifying glass on top of a surface while distorting the image below it. To add this bit of realism, take your effect one step further and create the distortion. The easiest way to see this effect is to view it against a lined background, which is why you used one for this exercise.

Command-click (Control-click on a PC) on the layer in the Layers palette to turn it into a selection (Figure 45).

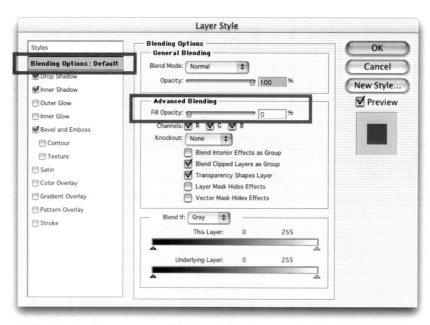

44 The Blending Options portion of the Layer Style dialog box. The Advanced Blending field is set.

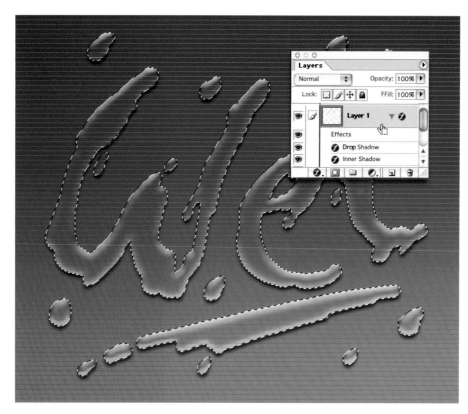

45 The layer with the word is turned into a selection.

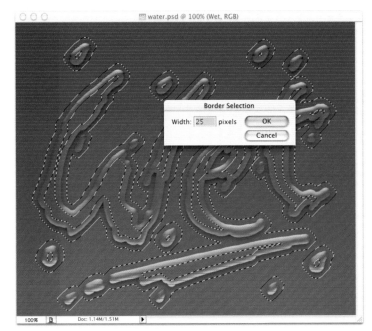

Choose Border from the Select menu (Select>Modify>Border). Give it a border large enough to resemble the one shown in Figure 46.

The effect you want to create employs the Displace filter. This filter is discussed in more detail in Chapter 8, "Bending Things a Bit." This filter requires a separate file in order to perform its function. Choose Save Selection from the Select menu and save it to a new document.

In the new document, choose the Gaussian Blur filter (Filter>Blur> Gaussian Blur). Choose a rate that is high enough to sufficiently blur the image without distorting it, as shown in Figure 47.

Save the document. Give it a name that distinguishes it from other files. I named my new file Map for Wet (Figure 48).

46 The Border command is used to create an outlined area of the selection.

47 The new document is blurred.

48 The new document is saved.

Back in the original image, make a duplicate of the Background layer (the gradient with lines). Select the duplicated layer so that it is the active layer (Figure 49).

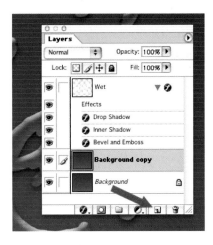

49 The Background layer with the blue gradient and line pattern is duplicated.

Select the Displace filter (Filter>Distort>Displace). Use the default settings for the Displace filter, and click OK (Figure 50).

The dialog box that opens asks you to select the Displacement Map, as shown in Figure 51. This is the image that is used to bend the pixels. Select the image you created from the alpha channel in Figure 48.

Now, you'll get rid of the excess image area in the distorted layer, so that the distortion is visible only in the water area. Activate the layer with the wet elements by Command-clicking (Control-A on a PC) on it in the Layers palette.

Choose Inverse from the Select menu. Make sure you are still in the copied Background layer or the layer with the distortion. Press Delete on your keyboard.

You are now finished. The result should look similar to the illustration shown in Figure 52.

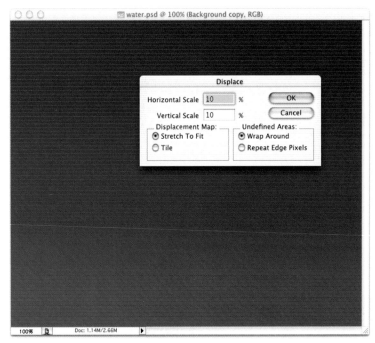

50 The Displace filter is employed.

51 The Displacement Map, previously created from the alpha channel, is chosen.

52 The final product.

Let It Snow

The process for creating snow is almost the same as the one used for creating rain, but it has fewer steps. This is interesting to note when you consider that in real life snow and rain are the same thing—the only difference is the temperature.

Figure 53 shows a scene in which the snow has already fallen. To complete the scene, I want to show the snow falling.

As you did previously in this chapter, create a new layer. Fill it with black, as shown in Figure 54.

53 I want to show falling snow for this scene.

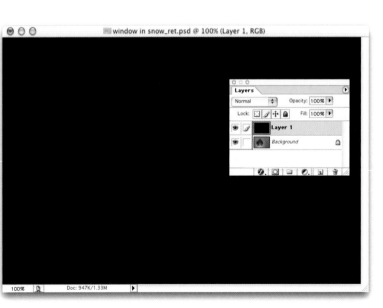

54 A new layer is created and filled with black.

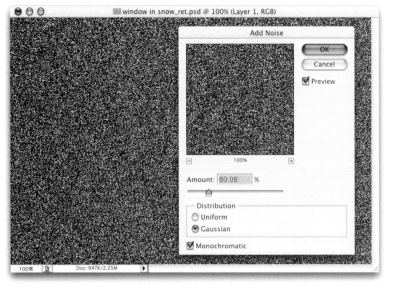

55 The Add Noise filter is applied to the layer.

The Add Noise filter (Filter>Noise>Add Noise) is applied (Figure 55). The Gaussian field is set to a high percentage.

The Noise layer is blurred next with the Gaussian Blur filter (Filter>Blur>Gaussian Blur). The radius amount should be enough to blur it, as shown in Figure 56.

The Levels command (Image>Adjustments>Levels) is used to increase the contrast between black and white, as shown in Figure 57.

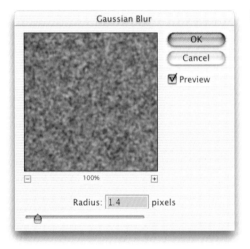

56 The Gaussian Blur filter is applied to the layer.

57 The Levels command increases the contrast.

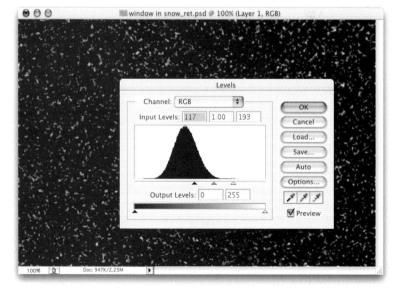

The layer with the modified noise is put in Screen mode so that only the white is visible (Figure 58). Snow falls much slower than rain; thus, the eye has a chance to decipher the shapes of the snow. What you want to show in this scene are the different shapes and sizes of the snowflakes.

To do this, the layer of snow is duplicated (Figure 59). Using the Zoom tool, the image is downsized so that you see the paste-board area outside the image proper. The duplicated Snow layer is enlarged beyond the image's margins with the Scale tool (Edit>Transform>Scale), as seen in Figure 60.

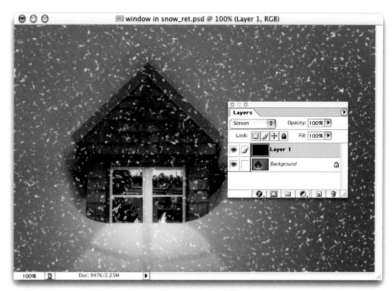

58 The layer is put into Screen mode.

59 The layer with the snow is duplicated.

60 The duplicated layer is scaled up.

NOTE   Although the scaled layer is outside of the image area, the information contained in it is still available. This is handy when you want to bring this file into a program such as Adobe After Effects, where you can animate individual Photoshop layers. Moving the layers of snow downward produces an effective animation. The original layer with the small snow is moved down at a slower pace than the scaled up layer that contains the larger snowflakes.

Figure 61 shows the final image with gentle snow falling.

61 The final scene of falling snow.

Where There's Smoke, There's Fire

Smoke and fire are two things that were somewhat difficult to create in earlier versions of Photoshop. These elements require a convoluted number of steps, not to mention a high degree of drawing skill. Liquify has changed this. In the last chapter, you saw how to create wooden textures using Liquify. In this chapter, it is used to create fire and smoke.

Figure 62 shows an image I created for a client in 2001. She is a renowned artist who has a sideline business of creating collectable shoes. These aren't the kind of shoes you wear, unless you have tiny feet, but they are the kind you display in a case or on a mantelpiece. She decided to take her original drawings of the shoes and place them in situations that complement the style of the shoe. The one shown here is called the Red Devil. It made sense to set it on fire.

62 The illustration for the Red Devil shoe.

Figure 63 shows the original pencil drawing. The final illustration is done in Photoshop. The process for the flames and smoke involve a couple of filters and the Liquify command.

To demonstrate the technique for creating fire and smoke, I'll walk you through the creation of a campfire scene. Figure 64 is the start of the campfire scene. Logs are created in the same fashion as the tree in Chapter 3, "A Greener World: Creating Foliage." The logs are in their own layer, and the Background layer is set to black.

63 This is the original pencil drawing of the Red Devil Shoe by the artist, Lorraine Vail.

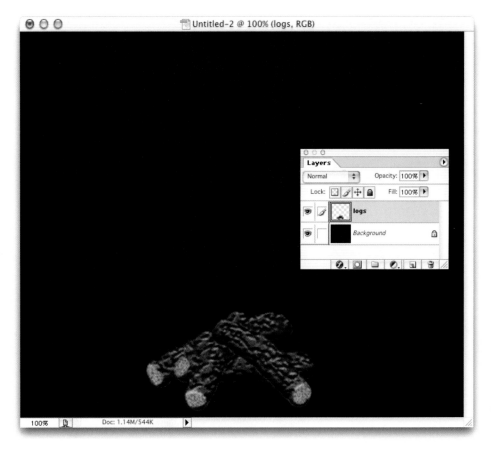

64 The campfire scene before someone strikes a match.

A new layer is created to contain the flames. Using a custom brush for grass, a few strokes are applied in white. These become the foundation for the flames. I used a Grass brush because the shape starts to resemble flames right from the start (Figure 65).

Duplicate the layer with the Grass strokes. The original layer is used later to form the foundation of the smoke. Its Eye icon is turned off to hide it. The next few steps are applied to the duplicated layer, not the original layer.

The first filter you apply works only from the left or from the right. To get the desired effect of flames shooting upward, rotate the layer 90 degrees clockwise. Then, apply the Wind filter from the Left (Filter>Stylize>Wind). Apply it a couple of times to get longer streaks, as seen in Figure 66.

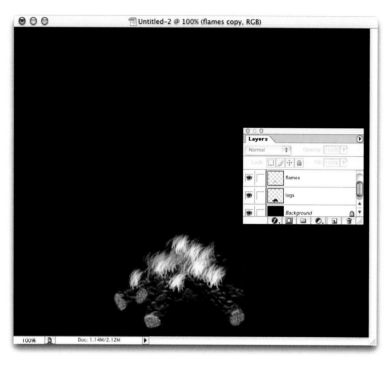

65 A few strokes with a Grass brush are applied to a layer to form the basis of the flame.

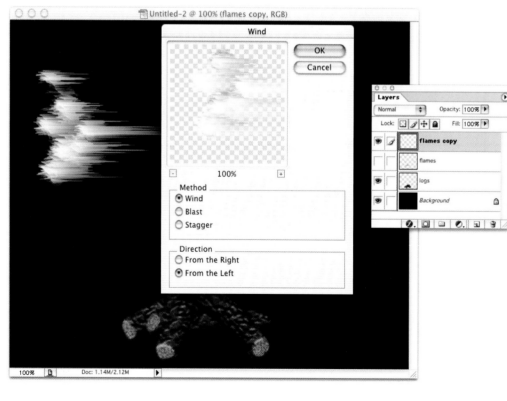

66 The Flame layer is duplicated and rotated. The Wind filter is then applied to it.

Rotate the layer back to its original, upright position. Apply the Gaussian Blur filter (Filter>Blur>Gaussian Blur). Note that you should give it just enough blur to soften the streaks, as shown in Figure 67.

NOTE I do not refer to the actual numbers used for the settings in the dialog boxes that appear in the images in this section. This is because these are not meant to be formulas. Your settings may differ based on the resolution of your file, and so on.

The Liquify filter displays the currently selected layer to be modified. In version 6, it is very difficult to see a white layer against the checkerboard pattern of the transparency indicator. Photoshop 7 enhances the Liquify command so that other layers are visible in the work area.

The flames are created in white, but when you distort them, you need to include black to offset the shapes. To get the black, create a new layer behind the layer of the flames and fill it with black. Then, choose Merge Down from the Layers palette menu. This unites the layer of the flames with the black-filled layer into a single layer (Figure 68).

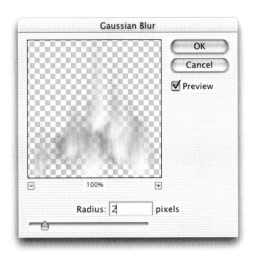

67 The Gaussian Blur filter is applied.

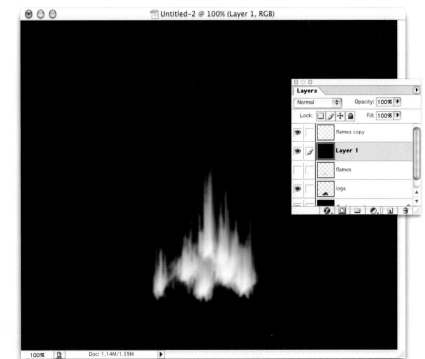

68 A layer filled with black is created behind the layer with the white flames, and then the two layers are merged into one.

Use the Warp and Turbulence tools in the Liquify filter to distort the streaks into flames, as shown in Figure 69.

When you are done, switch the mode of the layer to Screen. As you know, this exposes the untouched underlying image, of which the top layer is black. Use the Hue/Saturation command (Image>Adjustments>Hue/Saturation), and click the Colorize button to change the hue of the flames. Set it to a warm yellow color, as illustrated in Figure 70.

The result gives you yellow flames, which are shown in Figure 71.

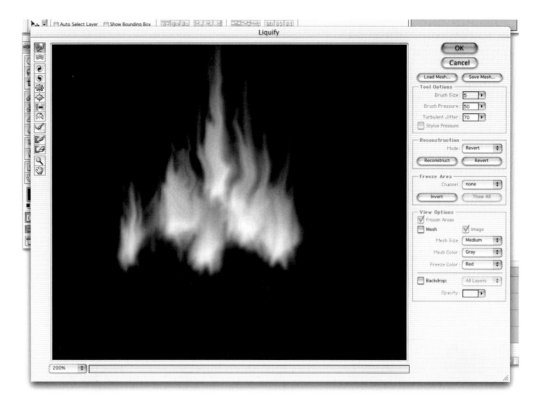

69 The flames are distorted in the Liquify filter.

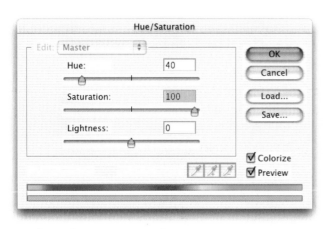

70 The Hue/Saturation command is used to colorize the white flames.

71 The result of the Hue/Saturation command's adjustment.

72 The Hue/Saturation
adjustment is made to
the duplicated layer.

If you duplicate the layer of the flames and then change
the Hue to –20, you change the yellow to more of an
orange color (Figure 72).

Set the mode of the duplicated layer to Color Dodge. This
introduces some red colors to the flames, as shown in
Figure 73.

73 The newly adjusted layer is
changed to Color Dodge mode.

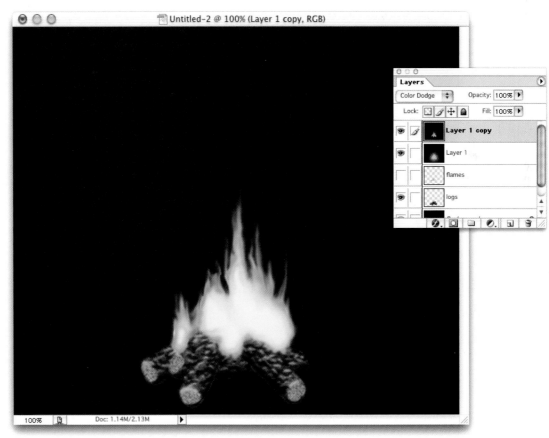

Go back to the layer with the original white brush strokes, which became the basis for the creation of the flames. Apply the Wind filter to them. I applied the filter twice as many times as I did for the flames. This gives you longer streaks, which serve as the foundation for the creation of the smoke. As done previously, the layer is merged with a black-filled layer and then brought into the Liquify filter. Again, using the Warp tool, stretch the shapes up and out. Apply a few strokes with the Turbulence tool. The results are shown in Figure 74.

The layer is then put into Screen mode and positioned over the flames (Figure 75).

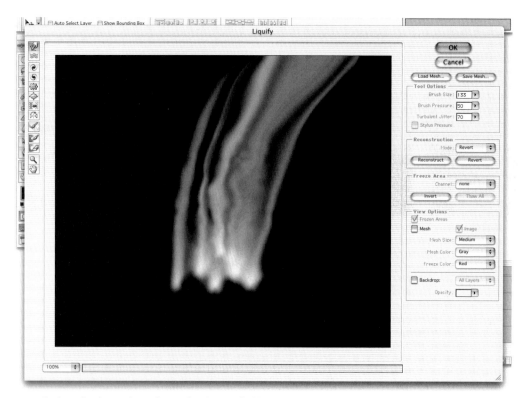

74 The layer for the smoke is distorted in the Liquify filter.

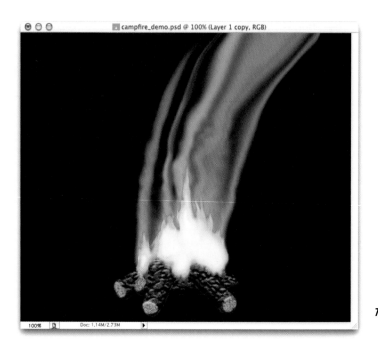

75 The smoke is now rising over the campfire.

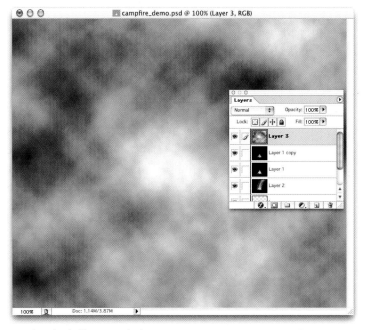

As smoke rises, it gets hung up in the wind or breeze, and it takes on new shapes as a result. To achieve this effect, you create a new layer on top of the other layers. With the Foreground and Background colors reset to Black and White, apply the Clouds filter to the layer (Filter>Render> Clouds). This produces a mass of clouds very much like the ones created for the stormy sky at the beginning of this chapter (Figure 76).

The layer is sized to fit into the upper part of the trailing smoke (Edit>Transform>Scale), as shown in Figure 77.

The layer with the clouds is set to Screen mode to hide the black in it. With a large-sized Eraser, I softened the edges to minimize the effect. Figure 78 shows the final campfire burning away.

76 The Clouds filter is applied to a new layer.

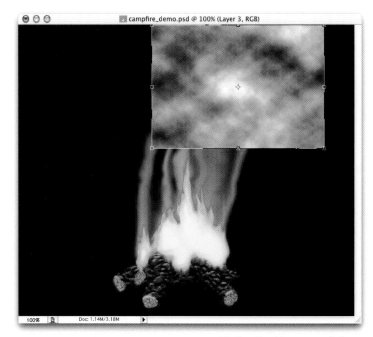

77 The Cloud layer is scaled to fit above the trailing smoke.

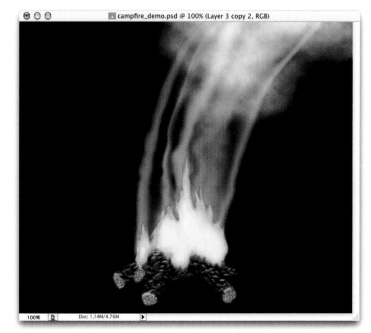

78 The final image of the campfire as it blazes away.

Feeling a Little Foggy?

You saw the use of the Clouds filter (Filter>Render>Clouds) earlier in this chapter. This filter is used for many things, but so far, you have seen it used for what it is named after—clouds. There is another phenomenon in nature that can really get up close and personal—fog.

The Clouds filter can easily create the shapes in a foggy scene. However, just like in the case of the rainy day, clouds alone do not make the whole picture.

Figure 79 is the same image you created in Chapter 3, "A Greener World: Creating Foliage." This is a bright and cheerful image of the tree. I live in Berkeley Hills, and fog is very common there. They don't call San Francisco the fog city for nothing. That fog just rolls in over the bay all the time.

79 The image of a tree on a clear day.

The fog is created in a layer above the other layers that make up the tree scene. Apply the Clouds filter with black and white in the new layer. Set it to Screen mode. Note that this is not enough. To re-create the effect, you have to set the mood. As you see in Figure 80, adding the clouds is not enough to create the effect of fog.

Each layer of the image is desaturated and lightened using the Hue/Saturation command. The trees behind the main tree are lightened more than the main tree. The trees off in the distance are lightened even more.

80 The image of the tree with the Clouds filter applied.

81 The layers are desaturated and lightened.

With these minor adjustments, the Clouds
filter creates the fog effect (Figure 82).

82 The image of the tree is now
   illustrated to look like it's
   shown on a foggy day.

7

Reflections

In Chapter 5, "What's It Made Of? Creating Textures," you learned how to create the materials that objects are made of, and in Chapter 4, "Lights and Shadows," you saw how objects cast shadows or have shadows cast onto them. There is another aspect to surfaces that needs to be addressed. The final aspect we need to address is how objects react to the world around them.

For example, assume that you created a wooden table using the techniques for wood discussed in Chapter 5. What if that table is supposed to be polished? Well, you'd get reflections, and reflections give an entirely different dimension to an object.

A reflection can basically be an object flipped in the opposite direction from which it is viewed. Sometimes you can select an object and choose Flip Horizontal (Edit>Transform>Flip Horizontal) to create a reflection. Typically, though, there are other factors involved. In this chapter, we explore many variations of reflections and how to make them.

The shape of an object that is catching a reflection is a major consideration. Angles distort the reflection. Perspective plays a key role.

Let's start with a simple reflection. In the image on the cover of this book, the surface of the dresser is polished (Figure 1). In Figure 2, the layer that contains the reflection was removed. This makes a difference, doesn't it?

1 A close-up of the cover image reveals a reflection on the polished surface of the dresser.

2 Removing the layer of the reflection changes the look of the dresser.

Creating the reflection is simple enough. The mirror and vase are simply duplicated and flipped vertically. The Motion Blur (Filter>Blur>Motion Blur) is applied in a vertical direction. The result of these modifications is seen in Figure 3. The opacity is lowered. Finally, the layer of the wooden dresser top is used to clip the layer of the reflection (Figure 4). It is not necessary to eliminate or distort the elements in the reflection because the cloth draped over the dresser hides most of them.

3 The objects that make up the reflection are duplicated, flipped vertically, and blurred.

4 The layer of the dresser's wooden top is used to clip the layer of the reflection.

5 The Layers palette shows the clipping group of the wooden top and the layers of the reflections.

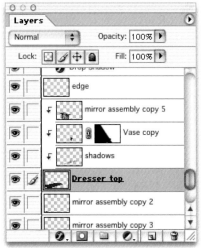

A Need for Change

The "Solano Grill" painting is a different story. The glass panes on the door reflect the menu box and its surrounding section of wall (Figure 6). However, because of the angle at which it is viewed, a simple duplicate-and-horizontal flip does not work. Doing this places the menu and its reflection at 90-degree angles to one another (Figure 7). In real life, because the door itself is perpendicular to the menu, the reflection must appear as an extension of the wall; it has to be parallel, not perpendicular to the original.

6 The "Solano Grill" painting shows a visible reflection in the glass panes on the door.

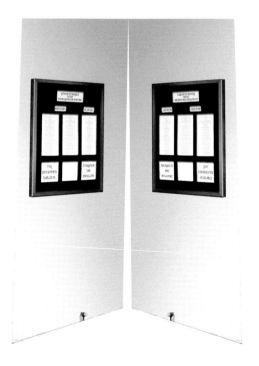

7 The layers containing the wall and menu box are duplicated and flipped horizontally.

This is a fairly simple procedure. Using the Distort function (Edit>Transform>Distort), the duplicated section of the wall is distorted to follow the angle of the original wall (Figure 8).

The display case with the menus requires a considerable amount of alteration to make it behave the way a real reflection does. For one thing, it is in full view within the reflection, so matching the perspective is crucial.

To do this, I created a new layer where I could map out guidelines to control the necessary distortion. With the Line tool, I drew lines that followed the vanishing lines of the menu case, as shown in Figure 9.

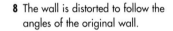

8 The wall is distorted to follow the angles of the original wall.

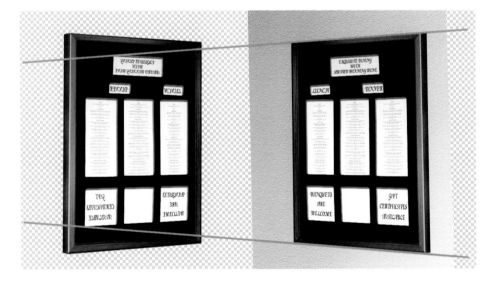

9 Guides are created to ensure the accuracy of the distortion of the menu box and to follow the perspective of the original.

10 The menu box is distorted to follow the direction of the guides.

Next, I used the Distort function (Edit>Transform>Distort) to distort the menu case in the same fashion as I did with the wall. The difference here is that I used the guides to guarantee proper alignment.

After I flipped the menu case, I faced a problem with its edges. The outside edge in both the menu and the reflection appears raised compared to the inside edge. For the actual menu box outside of the restaurant, this effect is correct. The viewer should see more of the outside edge. However, the inside edge is closer to the door, and that inside edge must be emphasized in the reflection, because the door is, in effect, looking at the menu from an angle that is opposite to the one seen by the viewer outside of the restaurant. In Figure 11, you see the edge on the left and the new edge on the right. In Figure 12, the left edge is removed.

11 The edge on the left side is facing the wrong direction. The new edge on the right side is correct.

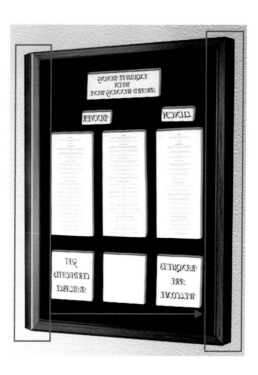

12 The left edge is erased.

This is not enough. Just like the edge of the case had to be changed, so did the edges of the menu on display in the case. In the original, the edges appear raised to the right; that is, they appear closer to the viewer. In the reflection, this is the wrong perspective. In Figure 13, these edges are transposed on the three center panels. Note that the remaining panels are facing the wrong way.

The doorstop is not visible in the reflection. I felt it would further emphasize the concept of reflections and that is that a simple flip horizontal is not always enough to make an effective reflection. Manipulation of the elements is required to achieve maximum realism. Figure 14 shows the doorstop as it appears in the image. Figure 15 shows what the reflection should look like. Notice the shadows on the right side. The side on which the hook appears has also been changed from right to left.

13 The edges on the three main panels are adjusted to conform to the angle of the reflection.

14 A close-up view of the doorstop.

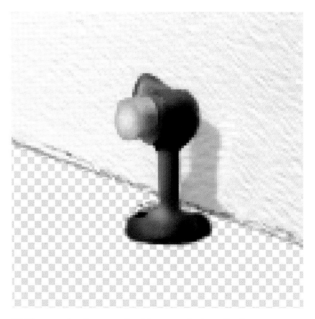

15 The way the doorstop should appear in the reflection.

16 The planter is placed in a layer behind the layer of the reflection. The planter is then scaled down.

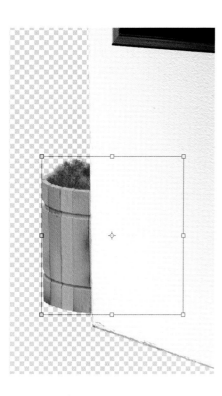

The planter on the side of the entrance is duplicated and placed in a layer behind the layer with the reflection of the wall. This creates the illusion that the wall partially hides it. It is then scaled down in size because the reflection appears farther from our point of view (Figure 16).

There is a reflection of a parked van that is visible in the window on the far right side of the painting (Figure 17). It is created as a separate image. The shape of the van is distorted to simulate the warped nature of the plate glass window that is in the actual scene. I actually created the van with the distortion as seen in Figures 18 and 19. If you use an existing image for a similar situation, you can use a distortion filter. Let's see an example of this.

17 A parked van is visible in the window.

18 The layer for the van is created as a series of filled shapes.

19 The layer of the van is merged with a layer behind it, which is then filled with black to form the reflection.

The painting, "The Alibi," includes a large neon sign. The metal sign with the word Breakfast on it is reflective (Figure 20). It reflects the neon sign. Like the door reflections in the "Solano Grill" painting, a simple Flip Horizontal is not enough to achieve the reflection.

20 The painting, "The Alibi," has a reflection that is visible on the right, behind the word Breakfast.

The layers that contain the neon tubes and the structure for the sign are duplicated and flipped, as shown in Figure 21. Using the Skew command (Edit>Transform>Skew), the layer that serves as the reflection is skewed to follow the angle of the sign, as shown in Figure 22.

There is still one very important consideration to deal with—perspective. The neon tubes are suspended over the sign, which creates a space between them. This space is noticeable depending on the viewing angle. Figure 23 demonstrates this concept.

In the diagram in Figure 23, the arrows signify the viewer's visual direction. If you look at the arrow (the view angle) on the left, you see the neon tube directly over the painted word behind it. The center arrow's angle provides a view of the neon tube slightly off of center to the right. The arrow at the far right provides a view into the reflection. In the reflection, the angle is so strong that a space appears to be between the neon tube and the painted letter behind it.

21 The layers containing the sign and neon are duplicated and flipped horizontally.

22 The layer with the reflection is skewed to follow the angle of the original sign.

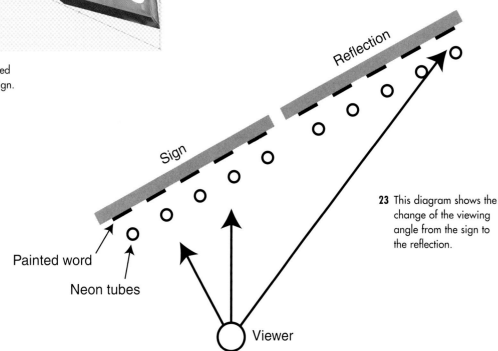

23 This diagram shows the change of the viewing angle from the sign to the reflection.

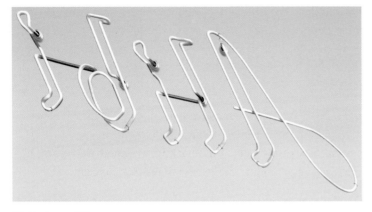

24 The layer of the neon.

To achieve this effect, I kept the layer that contained the neon (Figure 24) separate from the one that had the sign (Figure 25). I was then able to move the layer with the neon over slightly to simulate the view angle change (Figure 26). After I had the two layers in position, I merged them and distorted them using the Wave filter (Filter>Distort>Wave), as shown in Figure 27.

You will notice that not much care is taken in the original distortion of the neon tubes, as shown in Figure 24. Additional attention to details, such as where the tubes attach to the sign, is not necessary because the reflection is mostly obscured by the word Breakfast (Figure 28). The area of the reflection is also small.

25 The layer of the sign.

26 The layer of the neon is moved slightly to the right to simulate the viewing angle of the reflection.

27 The layer of the reflection is distorted using the Wave filter.

28 The reflection is visible through a small section of the metal sign.

There are times when it is necessary to take the extra step to make things look right. "The Sidelines" painting utilizes a neon sign, as shown in Figure 29. This time the tubes are reflected directly behind themselves on the face of the sign board.

30 The neon in this painting is reflected directly behind it on the surface of the sign.

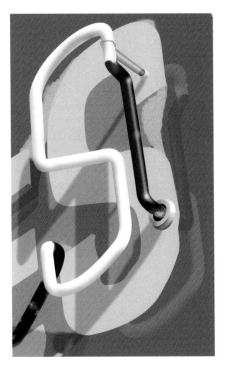

As in all the previous examples, the layer that is reflected is first duplicated. However, this time the duplicated layer that serves as the reflection is not flipped or skewed. It is simply moved to the right and down far enough to simulate the necessary distance of the neon tube from the surface of the sign it is mounted to. However, looking at the close-up in Figure 31, you see that there will have to be some modification. Because you are looking into the reflection, you should see the other side of the neon tubes. The bend in the tube as it enters the base of the sign should travel in the opposite direction.

To get this effect, I separated the pieces that needed to be altered and placed them into their own layer, as shown in Figure 32. In the layers, these individual pieces were then flipped and skewed to match the angles of the actual neon tubes (Figure 33).

The opacity is lowered considerably to make the reflection barely visible. If the surface of the sign had been a mirror, then the opacity would have had to remain at 100%.

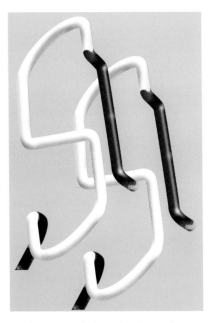

31 The neon is duplicated and moved over to match the position of the reflection.

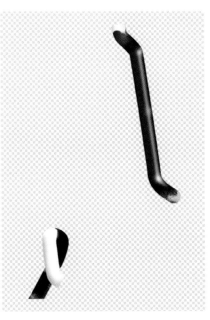

32 The parts of the neon that need to be altered are separated into their own layer.

33 The altered neon tubes follow the angles for a realistic reflection.

Easy Stuff

I thought I should include an easy reflection after the complicated, altered stuff. The "Altoids" image is of a breath mint case opened on a tabletop (Figure 34).

A close look inside the opened lid reveals a reflection (Figure 35). The metal is shiny and highly reflective.

34 The painting "Altoids."

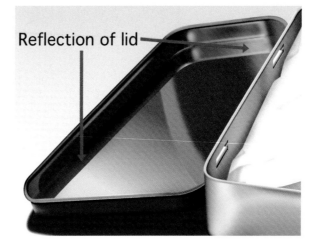

35 The lid section of the painting has a reflection of the lid visible in it.

We gladly accept returns of new and unread books and unopened music from bn.com with a bn.com receipt for store credit at the bn.com price.

Full refund issued for new and unread books and unopened music within 30 days with a receipt from any Barnes & Noble store.
Store Credit issued for new and unread books and unopened music after 30 days or without a sales receipt. Credit issued at lowest sale price.
We gladly accept returns of new and unread books and unopened music from bn.com with a bn.com receipt for store credit at the bn.com price.

Full refund issued for new and unread books and unopened music within 30 days with a receipt from any Barnes & Noble store.
Store Credit issued for new and unread books and unopened music after 30 days or without a sales receipt. Credit issued at lowest sale price.
We gladly accept returns of new and unread books and unopened music from bn.com with a bn.com receipt for store credit at the bn.com price.

In Figure 36, you see the layer containing the edge of the lid. I created it by making the shape with the Pen tool and filling it with colors. To create the reflection, the layer is duplicated and moved down, as shown in Figure 37. Blue and white highlights are introduced into the reflection to represent the light that spills over the edge.

The layer containing the face of the lid is activated so that you can see the reflection in place. The opacity for the layer with the reflection is lowered slightly to make the lid seem like something just short of an actual mirror (Figure 38).

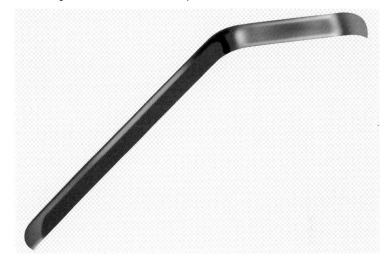

36 The edge of the lid is created in a layer.

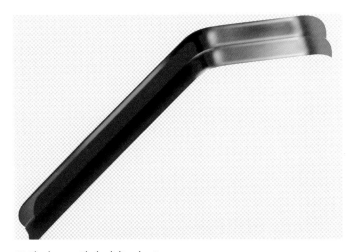

37 The layer with the lid's edge is duplicated and moved down to serve as the reflection of the edge that is inside the lid's face.

38 The opacity is lowered for the layer with the reflection.

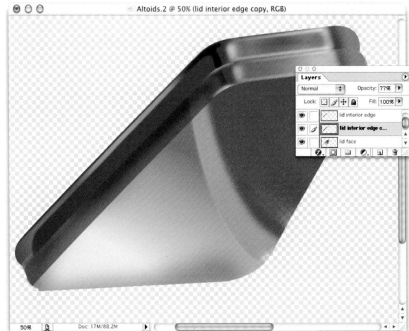

A Well-Rounded Understanding

The marble in the "matches and marble" painting picks up a reflection of the matchstick sitting next to it (Figures 39 and 40). The marble is made of a smooth glass that behaves like a mirror. Its rounded surface, a shape that distorts any reflection, complicates your life.

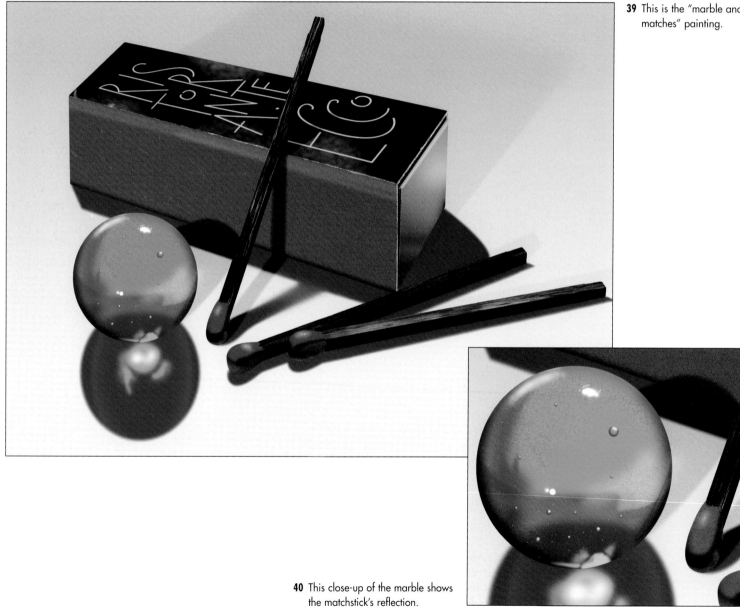

39 This is the "marble and matches" painting.

40 This close-up of the marble shows the matchstick's reflection.

The Spherize filter has been part of Photoshop since the early versions (Filter>Distort>Spherize). This filter basically bloats the central part of an image or selected area. It creates the illusion of an image wrapped around a sphere. The appropriate distortion is applied to the edges to give the foreshortening that completes the roundness of the object. In Figure 41, you see the before and after effect of the Spherize filter.

41 The image on the left is the original. The figure on the right has had the Spherize filter applied to it. Note the distortion of the edges. The darkening of the background in the image on the right is done to emphasize the effect for this example.

This distortion of the edges was the needed effect for the matchstick on the side of the marble.

I duplicated the layer that contained the matchstick over to a new file, as shown in Figure 42. It is necessary to keep the matchstick in a layer, so that the file is not flattened.

42 The matchstick is copied over to a new file.

The Spherize filter creates a sphere that is centered in the image. Knowing that the marble is a perfect sphere, I made the canvas of the file with the matchstick a perfect square. This guarantees that the distortion matches the shape of the marble. The reflection of the matchstick should appear on the right edge of the marble. I needed the distortion to appear along the right edge. To accomplish this, I placed the layer containing the matchstick at the far right of the window, as shown in Figure 43.

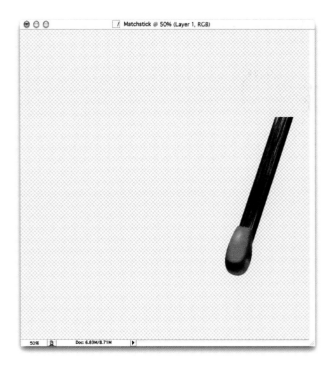

43 The matchstick is moved to the far right of the document window. This allows the filter to apply the appropriate distortion.

The Spherize filter was called into action, I gave it the full amount, and I applied it twice to maximize the effect (Figure 44).

The distorted matchstick's width is scaled down. This gives it the additional distortion needed to achieve realism.

I brought the layer of the distorted matchstick into the file with the marble (Figure 46). The layer that the match occupies was placed above the layer containing the marble so that it would be visible over the marble. I rotated and scaled the matchstick further to position it where I wanted the reflection to appear.

44 The Spherize filter is applied to the layer of the matchstick.

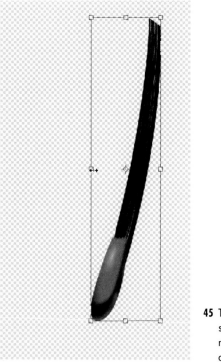

45 The matchstick is scaled down to make it thinner in appearance.

46 The layer with the matchstick is copied over to the file with the marble.

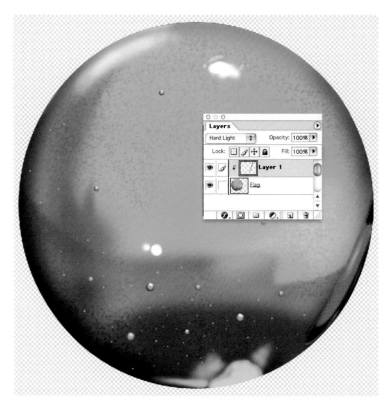

The layers of the marble and matchstick were turned into a clipping group (see Chapter 1, "Off to a Good Start"), as shown in Figure 47. Because the layer of the marble is under the layer of the match, its transparency information masks out the unwanted sections of the matchstick.

The opacity of the matchstick layer is lowered to allow the color of the marble to show through (Figure 48).

47 The layer with the matchstick and the layer of the marble are turned into a clipping group.

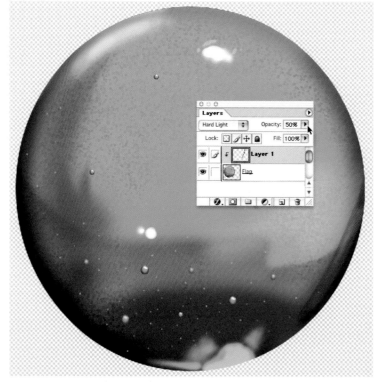

48 The opacity for the layer of the matchstick is lowered to complete the effect of the reflection.

Getting a Handle on Things

The "handles" image (Figure 49) is of a filing cabinet that sits directly below the counter that holds my computers. I was looking for something to paint one day during the rainy season. I laid my head down on the counter for a minute, and there it was!

© Bert Monroy 1998

49 The "handles" image is a picture of the filing cabinet under my desk.

If you look at close-ups of the handle areas for the top (Figure 50) and bottom (Figure 51), you see a configuration of strange shapes that make up the reflections.

The odd angle of the handles and their slim, curved surface make for an interesting study of reflections.

The shapes of the handles were created in Photoshop using the Pen tool (Figure 52).

In a separate layer for each handle, the paths are made into selections and filled with a solid gray color (Figure 53). I used a gray that was dominant in the overall color of the handle.

50 This is a close-up of the handle at the top of the filing cabinet.

51 This is a close-up of the handle at the bottom of the filing cabinet.

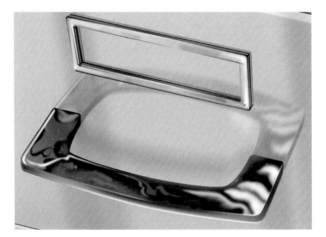

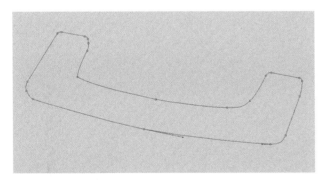

52 Shapes for the handles are created in Photoshop with the Pen tool.

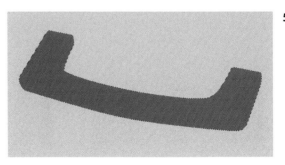

53 The paths are turned into selections and filled with a solid color.

Preserve Transparency was selected for the layers of the handles. Using the Paintbrush tool, I sprayed soft highlights along the edges with various shades of light grays (Figure 54).

With the Pen tool, wavy shapes were created to simulate the distorted patterns like the ones you see in the actual handles (Figure 55). These paths were made into selections with varying feather amounts to soften the edges. The selections were then filled with appropriate colors. In some cases, the selections were filled with gradients to create a sweeping highlight.

Some of the shapes for the various highlights were further distorted with the Smudge tool (Figure 56).

Dust and scratches were added in a separate layer with the Paintbrush tool.

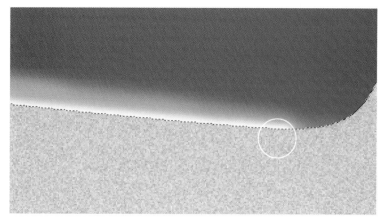

54 With the Paintbrush tool, highlights are added to the edges of the handles.

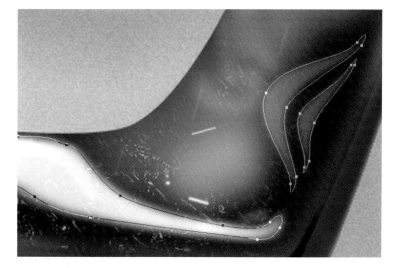

55 Shapes for the various highlights are created with the Pen tool.

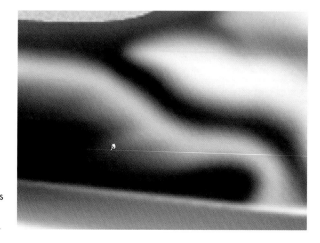

56 Some of the highlights are further distorted with the Smudge tool.

When each of the handles was completed, the layers that pertained to it were merged into a single layer. This merged layer was duplicated. This duplicated layer was to serve as the basis for the reflection of the handle on the face of the cabinet drawer.

The reflection layer was flipped, rotated, and skewed to follow the direction of the original handle. This made a mirror image of the handle (Figure 57).

Some additional distortion was required with the Distort feature (Edit>Transform>Distort) to match up the position of the reflected handle with the original handle (Figure 58).

The layer with the reflection was given a slight Motion Blur filter to soften the effect with a little streaking to the edges.

The opacity of the layer was then lowered. Finally, a layer mask was applied so the reflection would fade out as it got further from the face of the drawer (Figure 59).

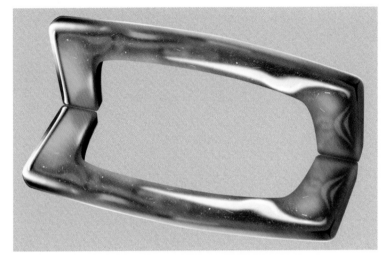

57 The duplicated handle is flipped, rotated, and skewed to match the angle of the original handle.

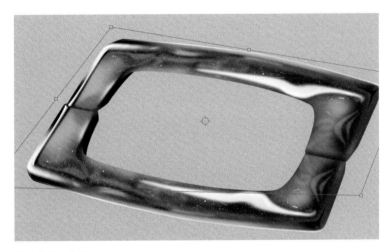

58 Additional distortion is required to properly match the position of the reflection.

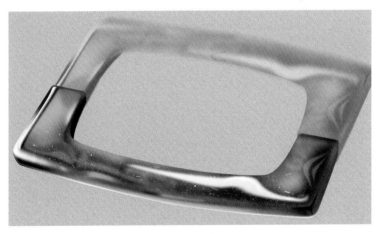

59 The opacity is lowered and a layer mask is applied to fade out the reflection.

The creation of shapes to represent distorted reflections can also denote the actual shape of the object.

The glass applicator in the image "ointment" is a prime example of this technique (Figure 60). In this case, the reflections outline the shape. With no reflections, the applicator appears as a flat, solid spoon.

60 The glass applicator is created with many different paths that are filled with varying colors.

61 The paths for the reflections on the glass applicator

8

Bending Things a Bit

Chapters 5, "What's It Made Of? Creating Textures," and 6, "Creating the Elements," demonstrate the use of the Liquify feature, a marvelous tool that is useful for bending and twisting parts of an image. As cool as it seems, Liquify does not solve all of your bending needs. There are times when you need total control over the direction that a pixel travels. This is when the Displace filter comes to the rescue.

The Displace filter works with two files. The first file is the image you want to distort, and the second file is the image that is used to distort the first image. The filter uses the luminosity values (lights and darks) of one image to distort another image. White or light gray values distort an image up and to the left. Black, or dark gray values, distort an image down and to the right. A 50% gray value has no displacement (distortion). The light and dark gray values distort the image based on the level of their intensity.

Keeping this in mind, you can create very elaborate displacement maps to distort images of every variety imaginable.

I often rely on the Displace filter for the creation of my paintings.

1 The Rendez-vous Café.

If you look at a close-up of the "Rendez-vous Café" image (Figure 1), you should notice the text that bends with the folds of the fabric of the awning over the restaurant's entrance (Figure 2).

2 Notice that the letters on the awning bend with the folds of the fabric.

If you look at the image during an early stage of production (Figure 3), you can see that the awning is missing the word COFFEES.

The text was created as straight text in Photoshop. I selected a font that closely matched the one that appeared on the awning of the actual restaurant. I typed in the word COFFEES. The text fell into its own layer as text (Figure 4). This layer of text could be edited at any time.

To perform the operations in this chapter, it was necessary to render the text layer. A rendered text layer enables you to manipulate individual characters (Layer>Rasterize>Type) of text. This is because the text is no longer text. Rendering the text converts it from vectors and curves into pixels that have a fixed resolution in Photoshop, as if it were a photograph.

I selected each of the individual letters. Using not the Displace function but the Distort function (Edit>Transform>Distort), the individual letters were distorted to simulate the wrap-around effect of the text on the awning. When you choose the Distort function, a box with handles appears around the selected object. Dragging these handles distorts the image in the direction of the drag. The letters in the "Rendez-vous Café" image were twisted downward. They were also scaled down and inward to give the impression of fading back in perspective (Figure 5). (You did read about perspective in Chapter 1, "Off to a Good Start," right?) The letters were then put into position around the edge of the awning.

At this point I needed to create the displacement map. This was the file that the filter used to distort the image.

I created an alpha channel in which to create my map. This allowed me to draw the map inside the image itself, which was necessary for proper positioning. To guarantee the proper alignment, I turned on the Eye icon for the RGB channels as I was working in the alpha channel. This allowed me to see the area that I was trying to match. The fact that the creation of the map was restricted to the alpha channel also ensured that the image would not be altered.

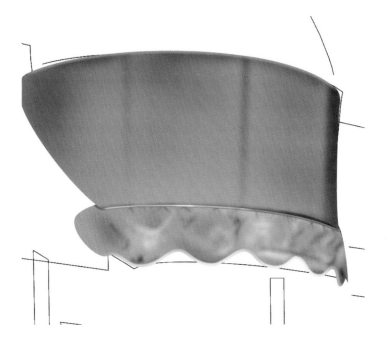

3 In this early version of the image, text is missing from the awning.

COFFEES

4 The text is created in its own layer using the Text tool.

5 The individual letters are distorted to follow the perspective of the awning.

I filled the alpha channel with a 50% gray. Over this gray, I added lighter tones to create the distortion. The gray color guaranteed that the rest of the image would not be distorted.

With the Paintbrush tool, I then created small wisps of light tones that would bend the text (Figure 6). When I did this, I had to remember that where whiteness appeared, the artwork would be distorted upward and to the left in those areas.

Next, I needed to make the displacement map image a file of its own. Because the majority of the files I work on are large (storage size), I usually do not depend on Copy and Paste to transfer image data. In the case of the alpha channel, I made it into a selection (Select>Load Selection). I then saved it to a new document (Select>Save Selection). In the Destination portion of the Save Selection dialog box, you can choose to save it to a new document. This works faster than copying and pasting it into a new file. It also makes me feel like a power user.

NOTE This procedure works well for large files. If you are working on small files, such as web images, then the Copy and Paste function works fine.

The file was then saved. Next, the alpha channel, in the original document, was deleted. The selection made to create the separate document was deselected.

The Displace filter was then applied (Filter>Distort>Displace) (Figure 7). The parameters in the Displace filter were lowered from the default of 10 to soften the effect (Figure 8).

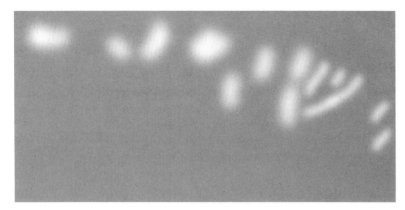

6 Small wisps of light tones are added with the Airbrush tool to form the areas for displacement.

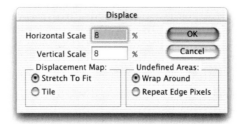

7 The Displace filter is applied.

8 In the Displace dialog box for the filter, the default setting is lowered to soften the effect.

The text then bends itself to the values set in the displacement map. This makes the letters look like they follow the folds on the awning, as shown in Figure 9.

The other words were distorted using the same method (Figure 10). In addition, new maps were created for each word.

COFFEES

9 The result is a text-bending effect, which gives the illusion that the distortion of the letters follows the folds in the fabric of the awning.

10 The other words in the scene are distorted in the same way.

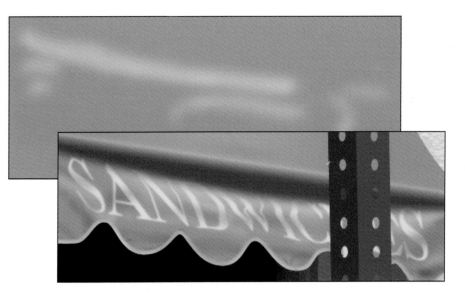

Shadows Cast on a Rough Surface

Shadows cast onto a rough or textured backdrop are distorted by the same texture to look believable. For example, the ripples in the sand in Figure 11 distort the edges of the shadow that the bottle casts. This effect is achieved with the Displace filter.

11 This image demonstrates the effect of a shadow that is cast across a rippled texture.

Each of the elements in the image in Figure 11 sits in its own layer. Duplicating the layer of the bottle and window frame created the shadow. The two duplicated layers were joined into a single layer (consult your Photoshop manual on how to merge layers). The layer was filled with black. It was blurred with the Gaussian Blur filter, and then distorted with the Distort function (Figure 12). See Chapter 4, "Lights and Shadows," for more information on creating shadows.

The Displace filter was selected. When the filter is applied, a dialog box first appears in which the parameters for the effect are set (Figure 13). When OK is clicked, an additional dialog box appears that asks for the displacement map.

The image of the desert existed as a separate file. When the filter requested a displacement map, the desert was used (Figure 14). The filter uses the Luminosity values of the desert (the lights and darks) to displace the pixels of the shadow.

12 The layer of the bottle and window frame is duplicated to create the shadow. The layer is filled with black, blurred, and then skewed.

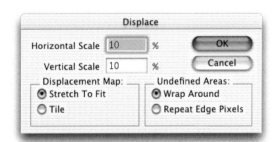

13 When the Displace filter is applied, the Displace dialog box appears in which parameters for the effect are set.

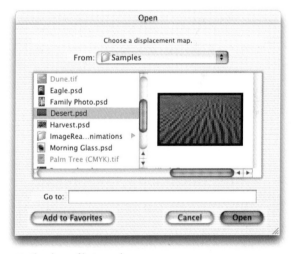

14 The desert file is used as a displacement map.

The final effect shows that the shadow was distorted to follow the ripples in the sand (Figure 15).

Notice that the shadow is not displaced where it crosses the road, which is flat. Unfortunately, the Ripple layer is continuous, uninterrupted by the road. This caused wiggles in undesirable places. To solve this, I created a second copy of the Shadow layer before applying the Displace filter to the original Shadow layer. I put the displaced shadow under the Road layer, and the untouched shadow on top of the road. Then, I changed the Road layer and the untouched shadow into a clipping group (Figure 16). To do this I clicked between the two layers in the Layers palette with the Option key (or Alt key) depressed. The transparency information in the Road layer masked out the shadow above it. In this way, the untouched shadow on the top replaces the shadow on the bottom only where it crosses the road.

If you are uncomfortable with clipping groups, you can also create the shape of the road as a 50% gray area in the displacement map before applying the displacement to the Shadow layer.

15 The final effect shows that the shadow is distorted to follow conforms to the ripples in the sand.

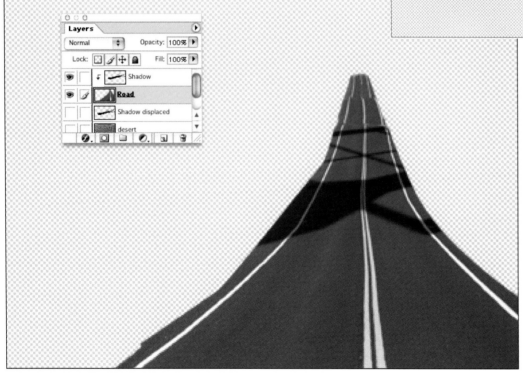

16 The layer of the road is turned into a clipping group with the layer of the shadow.

Flag Waving

To help you fully understand this extremely helpful Displace filter, we are going to create something together. We are going to simulate the third dimension from a flat, two-dimensional image. This will require the bending of the image.

To start, scan or create a picture of a flag. We are going to show the flag waving in the wind.

Put the flag in its own layer. Fill the Background layer with a blue gradient to represent the sky, as shown in Figure 17.

Create a new layer above the flag by clicking the Make New Layer icon at the bottom of the Layers palette (Figure 18).

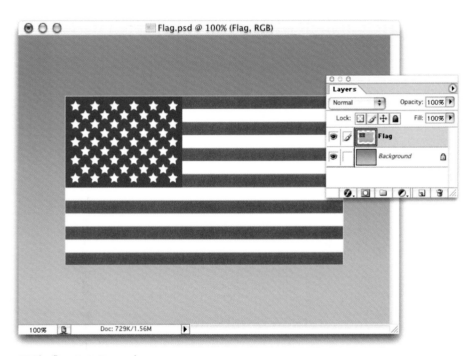

17 The flag sits in its own layer with a blue gradient in the Background layer.

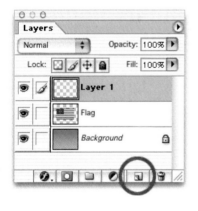

18 A new layer is created above the layer of the flag.

Fill this layer (Edit>Fill) with a 50% gray (Figure 19). Lower the opacity slightly for the gray-filled layer so that you can see the layer underneath the flag (Figure 20).

Using a large, soft-edged Paintbrush tool, spray some black tones across the flag, as seen in Figure 21. Do the same thing with a white color, as shown in Figure 22. Return the opacity for the layer to 100%. You might want to soften the tones a bit by giving the layer a Gaussian Blur filter (Filter>Blur>Gaussian Blur), as shown in Figure 23.

As stated previously, the filter needs a separate image to do its trick. Select all and then copy it to the Clipboard. Create a new file (Photoshop creates a file with the exact same dimensions of the contents of the clipboard), use the Paste command and paste everything into the new file, and then save the file.

19 The layer is filled with a 50% gray.

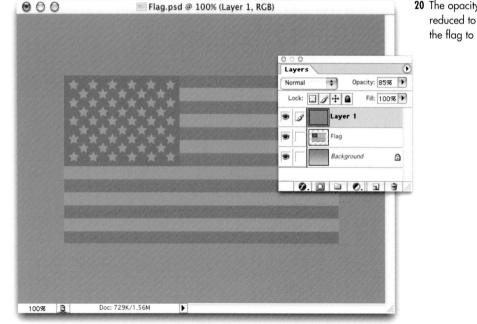

20 The opacity for the layer is reduced to allow the layer with the flag to show through.

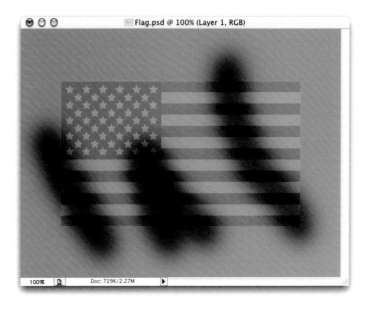

21 Black tones are added to the layer.

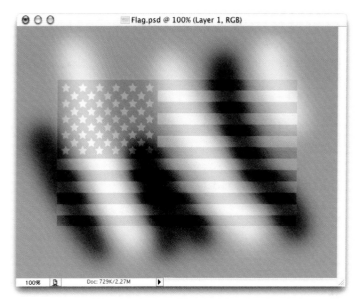

22 White tones are added to the layer.

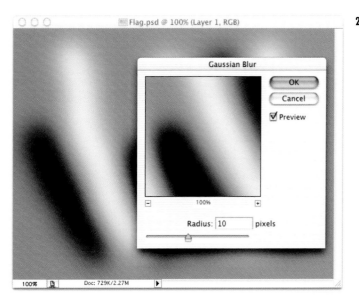

23 The layer is blurred to soften the paintbrush strokes.

In the file with the flag, select the layer with the flag, and turn off the Eye icon for the layer with the airbrushed tones in it to hide it. Choose the Displace filter (Filter>Distort>Displace). Leave the settings as they are and select OK. A second dialog box pops up asking for the displacement map. Choose the image you created for the map. The result should look like Figure 24.

It is difficult, especially if you haven't had a lot of practice, to get the displacement map exactly right the first time. Creating waves in the flag in this manner is definitely a move in the right direction; however, you can easily overdo it. You can use the Edit/Fade command to create a more conservative rippling effect. Reducing the opacity in the dialog box moves the filtered version back in the direction of the original.

There is a problem with Figure 24. The ripples work fine, but the lighting now seems inappropriate. The stripes should be lighter where they are closer to us, and they should be darker where the flag has rippled backward. Selecting the layer with the strokes and changing its mode offers the solution.

Hard Light, Soft Light, and Overlay all work on a principle somewhat similar to that of a displacement map. If the layer is 50% gray, there is no change in what is in the layers underneath. If the layer is something else—instead of distorting as the displacement map does—these three modes (I happen to have used Hard Light here, but others work as well) lighten or darken the underlying image depending on whether the top layer is lighter or darker than 50%. Therefore, by changing the mode to Hard Light, you can continue to use the same layer that created the original displacement map. This time, however, it lightens the forward areas of the flag closer to the viewer.

24 The layer of the flag is displaced.

25 The layer with the paint-brush strokes is selected and its mode is changed to Hard Light. The opacity is lowered.

This results in two issues. First, the effect is excessive, which is easily remedied by lowering the layer opacity, as shown in Figure 25. More importantly, because the brush strokes on the Hard Light layer goes beyond the boundaries of the flag, parts of the sky are lightened and darkened. We do not want that to happen, so you must set the Flag layer to clip the Hard Light layer (Figure 26) exactly as you did previously with the road and the shadow in Figure 16.

26 The layer is clipped by the layer with the flag.

Finally, merge the two layers into one and distort the layer (Edit>Transform>Distort) into a shape that is similar to the one shown in Figure 27. The end result is a flag waving in the wind (Figure 28).

27 The layer is distorted.

28 The final image is a flag waving in the wind.

The Gallery

Welcome to the gallery of the book. In these pages, I share with you some of my work that did not make it into the examples in the book. In the last book I published, I presented a trip down memory lane in the gallery by inserting images that dated back to the days when MacPaint was still being used. This book, however, is a Photoshop-only book. There is only one painting that is not a Photoshop file. It is the first painting in the gallery.

I did not include any of my commercial work. I feel a gallery should include just my fine art. If you want to see other stuff, you are more than welcome to visit my web site at **www.bertmonroy.com**. The site is frequently updated with new work.

As for this gallery, it shows more examples of the various techniques I covered in the book. I trust you can figure out how I created most of the pieces in here.

I put the art in chronological order. As you turn the pages, you can see the differences among the pieces as time passed. The machines got faster and stronger. Photoshop got more powerful.

I hope you enjoy the gallery. My hope is that it inspires you to explore your own capabilities. Whatever your subject matter, whatever your style, may you experience all the joy and passion of letting your imagination and creativity run wild.

The Subway Inn (1989)

The Subway Inn is one of those places that seems to have always been around and always will be. It's a dive of a place located behind Bloomingdale's loading docks in Manhattan. When I attended the High School of Art & Design, located a few blocks away, this place was already old.

This painting was actually created primarily with PixelPaint. PixelPaint was the first color paint program for the Macintosh II. I felt I could include this painting in the gallery because it repre-

sents the first time I incorporated Photoshop into a painting, though it was not yet commercially available at the time that I painted it.

At the time, Photoshop did not have many tools that could compare to the power of PixelPaint, but it had the greatest Airbrush tool. I used it to create the dirt on the signs and the walls. As I mentioned previously in the book, Jerry Harris, one of the co-creators of PixelPaint, wrote the fabulous Paint Engine in Photoshop 7.

Objects on Cloth (1989)

This painting represents an early Photoshop experiment in reflections and light refraction. The objects are just a bunch of items I had hanging around the house. I set the objects next to my computer and painted them "from life."

©Bert Monroy
'90

Lock (1990)

This represents more stuff I had from around the house. I am fascinated by reflective objects and competing textures.

© Bert Monroy '90

Sam's (1990)

Sam's is a great little Italian restaurant in Brooklyn. This painting is limited, but it's a long way from MacPaint. This was one of the first Photoshop paintings that I published. It appeared in *MacWeek* magazine.

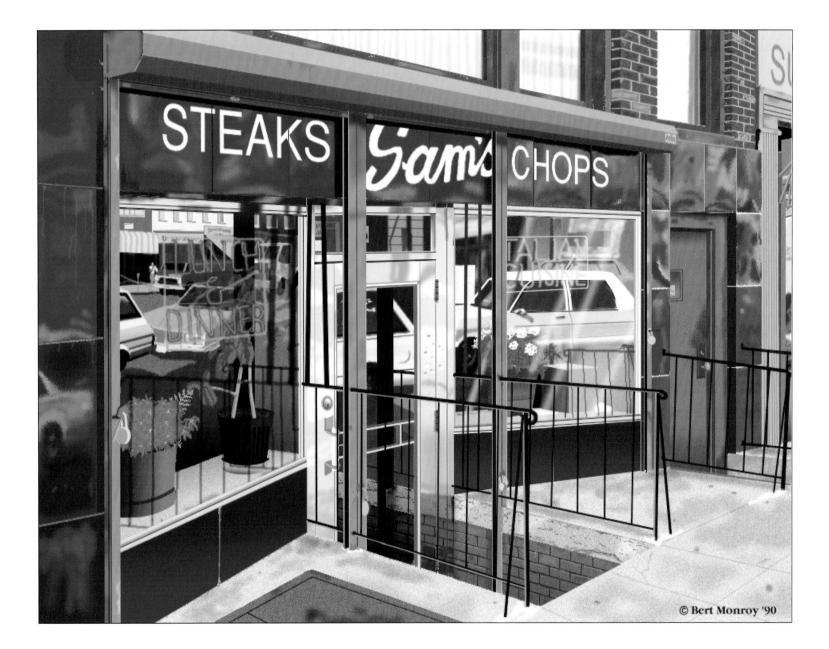

Height's Deli (1990)

What can I say? Brooklyn provided me with a lot of source material. This painting has such low resolution, you can see the pixels.

© BERT MONROY
1990

Sphere Chamber (1990)

An early experiment in reflections. Things were so much different then.

Nail Enamel (1991)

Though this was originally a commercial piece it has become a favorite of mine and of a few other people. Though I created hundreds of illustrations for Clinique, this one hangs on the walls of a few offices and homes.

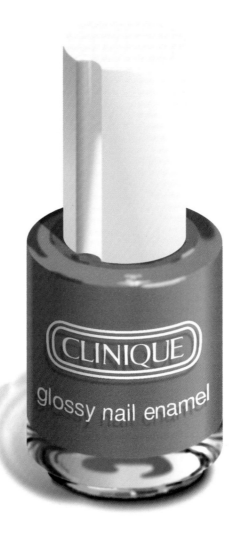

Zanzibar Motel (1991)

I just had to paint this one. This is a motel that is located across from a hotel I was staying at in Reno, Nevada. I was there teaching a class in Illustrator to the people who do the art you see on slot machines.

Hayden Orpheum (1991)

Haden Orpheum is the movie house across the street from the hotel where my wife and I were staying in Sydney, Australia.

Peter's Ice Cream (1991)

Peter's Ice Cream is one of those long-gone places in Brooklyn. It was the home of "Chocolate Decadence."

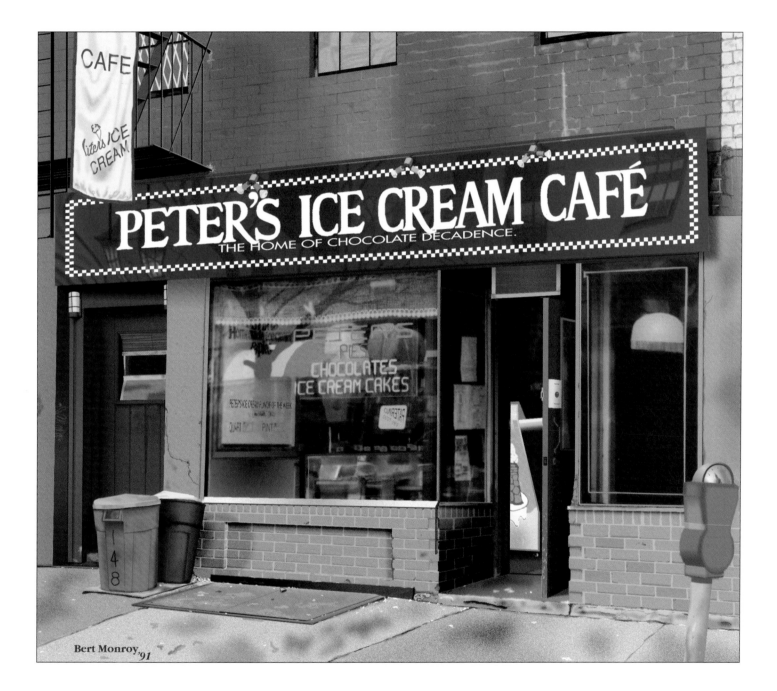

Abraham's Automotive (1992)

This is one of those places that jumped out at me and begged to be painted. We were on our way to the mountains outside of Sydney, Australia. I yelled out to stop the car so that I could jump out and take a few photographs of the place for reference.

Parkers' (1992)

That's the Manhattan Bridge in the background. Yep! You guessed it—we're back in Brooklyn.

The NY Deli (1993)

This is the last painting I did of a New York City subject. In 1993, we moved to California. This was painted in California from resource photographs that I had taken in New York.

© Bert Monroy 1993

Akihabara (1994)

This is of the electronics district in Tokyo. It is a colorful place bustling with throngs of people. No, I didn't get there before the crowds; I just didn't paint them.

Bean Bins (1994)

This is outside of the Tokyo Fish Market at
five o'clock in the morning.

Pic-n-Pac (1995)

This is of a convenience store I passed on the way home from the highway. This is my first California painting. The building has been repainted, but the store still looks the same.

Miller (1996)

In this painting, you can see that the fresh air and greenery of California are starting to get to me. These two trees were located down the street from my house. Unfortunately, they are no longer there.

© Bert Monroy 1996

View 2 (1996)

This was inspired by the evening walks my wife and I take. Look closely, and you will see the Miller trees repurposed.

© Bert Monroy 1996

Subway Seat (1998)

Inspiration can come from anywhere. I was visiting New York, where my sister lives, at the last stop of the No. 2 train. When you board a train going to the city, and you're at the first stop, you wait there for a while. I sat there and stared at the empty seat in front of me.

© Bert Monroy 1998

Window in Krakow (1998)

This window caught my attention on a trip to Poland. The sun hit
it in such a way that I felt it told me many stories of the past.

Studio Theater (1999)

I was captivated by this empty theater, which I saw on one of my trips to San Jose when visiting the folks at Adobe. It seemed ironic that the pole in front sported a banner advertising a film festival.

The Raven (1999)

I could not resist this colorful little movie house in the town of Healdsburg, California. Healdsburg is a great little town to visit. We love to eat next door at The Ravenous restaurant.

© Bert Monroy 1999

Hotel Arcata (2000)

The town of Arcata is one of those university California towns. In the book, you see The Sidelines and The Alibi, both bars on the same block as the hotel.

© Bert Monroy 2000

© Bert Monroy 2000

Little Church (2000)

This little church is located somewhere between Bodega Bay and Guerneville. We were headed inland to find the sun and to get away from that good old fog!

Streetlight (2000)

This is the view from the deck off of my bedroom. There is a streetlight that in wintertime, when the fruit trees are leafless, casts a glow across the deck.

© Bert Monroy 2000

Tower with a Weathervane (2000)

This was a doodle. I was just in the mood to knock something out that I had seen during an evening walk. This is the only place this image appears. It is not in any magazine or my web site.

AnyM (2001)

This place is actually an Any Mountain outlet in Berkeley. It was once the site of a wonderful produce store called Berkeley Bowl that has since moved across the street. It was originally a bowling alley, hence the name, Berkeley Bowl.

© Bert Monroy 2001

HAMBURGERS (2002)

When Adobe announced Photoshop 7, they did it at the PMA show in Orlando, Florida. They sent me there to participate in the festivities. The town is like one big amusement park. This place caught my eye and I had to paint it. I started it immediately after completing the writing of this book. Fortunately there was time to get it into the gallery.

Index

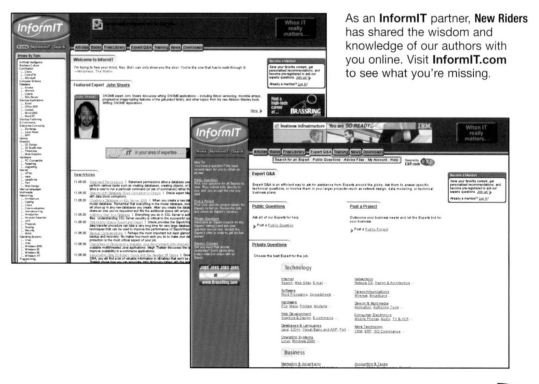

Publishing
the Voices
that Matter

web development | **graphics & design** | **server technology** | **certification**

You already know that New Riders brings you the Voices that Matter. But what does that mean? It means that New Riders brings you the Voices that will challenge your assumptions, take your talents to the next level, or simply help you better understand the complex technical world we're all navigating.

Visit **www.newriders.com** to find:

- ▶ Previously unpublished chapters
- ▶ Sample chapters/excerpts
- ▶ Author bios
- ▶ Contests
- ▶ Up-to-date industry event information
- ▶ Book reviews
- ▶ Special offers
- ▶ Info on how to join our User Group program
- ▶ Inspirational galleries where you can submit your own masterpieces
- ▶ Ways to have your Voice heard

New Riders

WWW.NEWRIDERS.COM

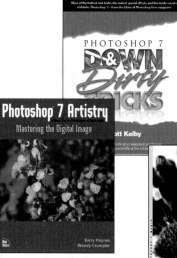

**Photoshop 7
Down & Dirty Tricks**
Scott Kelby
0735712379
$39.99

Photoshop 7 Magic
Sherry London,
Rhoda Grossman
0735712646
$45.00

Photoshop 7 Artistry
Barry Haynes,
Wendy Crumpler
0735712409
$55.00

Photoshop 7 Killer Tips
Scott Kelby
0735713006
$39.99

Inside Photoshop 7
Gary Bouton, Robert Stanley,
J. Scott Hamlin, Daniel Will-Harris,
Mara Nathanson
0735712417
$49.99

**Photoshop Studio with
Bert Monroy**
Bert Monroy
0735712468
$45.00

**Photoshop
Restoration and Retouching**
Katrin Eisemann
0789723182
$49.99

**Photoshop Type Effects
Visual Encyclopedia**
Roger Pring
0735711909
$45.00

**Creative Thinking in
Photoshop**
Sharon Steuer
0735711224
$45.00

New
Riders

VISIT OUR WEB SITE

WWW.NEWRIDERS.COM

On our web site, you'll find information about our other books, authors, tables of contents, and book errata. You will also find information about book registration and how to purchase our books, both domestically and internationally.

EMAIL US

Contact us at: **nrfeedback@newriders.com**

- If you have comments or questions about this book
- To report errors that you have found in this book
- If you have a book proposal to submit or are interested in writing for New Riders
- If you are an expert in a computer topic or technology and are interested in being a technical editor who reviews manuscripts for technical accuracy

Contact us at: **nreducation@newriders.com**

- If you are an instructor from an educational institution who wants to preview New Riders books for classroom use. Email should include your name, title, school, department, address, phone number, office days/hours, text in use, and enrollment, along with your request for desk/examination copies and/or additional information.

Contact us at: **nrmedia@newriders.com**

- If you are a member of the media who is interested in reviewing copies of New Riders books. Send your name, mailing address, and email address, along with the name of the publication or web site you work for.

BULK PURCHASES/CORPORATE SALES

If you are interested in buying 10 or more copies of a title or want to set up an account for your company to purchase directly from the publisher at a substantial discount, contact us at 800-382-3419 or email your contact information to corpsales@pearsontechgroup.com. A sales representative will contact you with more information.

WRITE TO US

New Riders Publishing
201 W. 103rd St.
Indianapolis, IN 46290-1097

CALL/FAX US

Toll-free (800) 571-5840
If outside U.S. (317) 581-3500
Ask for New Riders
FAX: (317) 581-4663

National Association of Photoshop Professionals

The only tool you need to master Adobe® Photoshop®

If you use Photoshop, you know that it's never been more important to stay up to date with your Photoshop skills as it is today. That's what the National Association of Photoshop Professionals (NAPP) is all about, as we're the world's leading resource for Photoshop training, education, and news. If you're into Photoshop, you're invited to join our worldwide community of Photoshop users from 106 different countries around the world who share their ideas, solutions, and cutting-edge techniques. Join NAPP today—it's the right tool for the job.

NAPP MEMBER BENEFITS INCLUDE:

- Free subscription to *Photoshop User*, the award-winning Adobe Photoshop "how-to" magazine

- Exclusive access to NAPP's private members-only Web site, loaded with tips, tutorials, downloads, and more

- Discounts on Photoshop training seminars, training videos, and books

- Free Photoshop tech support from our Help Desk and Advice Desk

- Get special member deals on everything from color printers to software upgrades to Zip disks, and everything in between

- Print and Web designers can earn professional certification and recognition through NAPP's new certification program

- Learn from the hottest Photoshop gurus in the industry at PhotoshopWorld, NAPP's annual convention

The National Association of Photoshop® Professionals
The Photoshop® Authority

One-year membership is only $99 (U.S. funds)
Call 800-738-8513 (or 727-738-2728)
or enroll online at **www.photoshopuser.com**

For more info on NAPP, visit www.photoshopuser.com

Corporate and International memberships available.
Photoshop and Adobe are registered trademarks of Adobe Systems, Inc.